P9-DFI-817

The Laws of
LIFETIME
GROWTH

ALWAYS MAKE YOUR FUTURE
BIGGER THAN YOUR PAST

Dan Sullivan
Catherine Nomura

The Laws of
LIFETIME
GROWTH

ALWAYS MAKE YOUR FUTURE
BIGGER THAN YOUR PAST

Second Edition
Updated and Expanded

BK

Berrett–Koehler Publishers, Inc.
a BK Life book

Copyright © 2007, 2016 by Strategic Coach, Inc.

Strategic Coach®, Unique Ability®, The 4 C's Formula™, The Strategic Coach® Program, The Strategic Coach® Signature Program, The 10x Ambition Program™, and The Growth Focuser™ and The Laws of Lifetime Growth® are trademarks, protected by copyright, and integral concepts of The Strategic Coach, Inc. All rights reserved.

†Genius Network® is a registered trademark of Piranha Marketing, Inc. All rights reserved.

††Protected Tomorrows® is a registered trademark of Protected Tomorrows, Inc.

All rights reserved. No part of this publication may be reproduced, distributed, or transmitted in any form or by any means, including photocopying, recording, or other electronic or mechanical methods, without the prior written permission of the publisher, except in the case of brief quotations embodied in critical reviews and certain other noncommercial uses permitted by copyright law. For permission requests, write to the publisher, addressed "Attention: Permissions Coordinator," at the address below.

Berrett-Koehler Publishers, Inc.
1333 Broadway, Suite 1000
Oakland, CA 94612-1921
Tel: (510) 817-2277   Fax: (510) 817-2278   www.bkconnection.com

Ordering Information
Quantity sales. Special discounts are available on quantity purchases by corporations, associations, and others. For details, contact the "Special Sales Department" at the Berrett-Koehler address above.
Individual sales. Berrett-Koehler publications are available through most bookstores. They can also be ordered directly from Berrett-Koehler: Tel: (800) 929-2929; Fax: (802) 864-7626; www.bkconnection.com
Orders for college textbook/course adoption use. Please contact Berrett-Koehler: Tel: (800) 929-2929; Fax: (802) 864-7626.
Orders by U.S. trade bookstores and wholesalers. Please contact Ingram Publisher Services, Tel: (800) 509-4887; Fax: (800) 838-1149; E-mail: customer.service@ingrampublisherservices.com; or visit www.ingrampublisherservices.com/Ordering for details about electronic ordering.

Berrett-Koehler and the BK logo are registered trademarks
of Berrett-Koehler Publishers, Inc.

Printed in the United States of America

Berrett-Koehler books are printed on long-lasting acid-free paper. When it is available, we choose paper that has been manufactured by environmentally responsible processes. These may include using trees grown in sustainable forests, incorporating recycled paper, minimizing chlorine in bleaching, or recycling the energy produced at the paper mill.

Library of Congress Cataloging-in-Publication Data

Names: Sullivan, Dan, 1944- author. | Nomura, Catherine, 1967- author.
Title: The laws of lifetime growth : always make your future bigger than your
    past / Dan Sullivan, Catherine Nomura.
Description: Second Edition. | Oakland : Berrett-Koehler Publishers, Inc.,
    2016. | Updated and revised edition of The laws of lifetime growth,
2006.
    | Includes index.
Identifiers: LCCN 2015047988 | ISBN 9781626566453 (pbk.)
Subjects: LCSH: Success.
Classification: LCC BJ1611.2 .S78 2016 | DDC 158--dc23
LC record available at http://lccn.loc.gov/2015047988

Cover Design: Mark van Bronkhorst, MvB Design
Book Production: Adept Content Solutions

To Babs and Hilda

Contents

Preface

The Growth Mindset

This is a very short book about a very big subject. The reason it can be so short and still be effective is that it works at the level of mindset, where change can happen in an instant, at the speed of thought. If you've ever had an "aha" moment that changed your thinking from that point forward, you know what we're talking about. What we've discovered in our work is that growth is a function of mindset. Change your thinking, and in moments you can go from not growing to growing, which we define as making your future bigger than your past.

The other reason it can be short is that you've done this before. We all have lots of experience to draw on when it comes to growth. Because we can remember what it feels like, we can do it again, we can do it in new areas, and we can learn to do it consciously and at will, as long as we can get into the right frame of mind.

Today, even more than in 2006 when this book first came out, having a growth mindset is not just an extraordinary advantage; it's often the difference between struggling and thriving. The world is changing faster than ever, which offers an abundance of challenges and opportunities. Some people choose to shut down in the face of uncertainty and change, while others blossom. The difference is mindset. If you're looking for an abundance of opportunities to grow that lead to great rewards, this is a tremendous time to be alive, but you need to be thinking about things in a way that lets you see and maximize the opportunities around you. The Laws of Lifetime Growth will help you do this. They can help you find your own growth path in what might otherwise seem like an overwhelming sea of opportunity by simply keeping your focus on growing day by day, week by week, continuing to make progress towards a bigger future that is all your own and endlessly fascinating and motivating.

You might wonder where these laws come from and how we're able to define a growth mindset in just ten short statements. The answer lies in the unique perspective gained from our work in the world of highly successful, achievement-oriented entrepreneurs. Though they come from many different backgrounds and parts of the world and their goals are equally diverse, these entrepreneurs all share one thing that they had long before we met them: a desire to grow that has propelled them to unusual levels of achievement. However, many entrepreneurs become trapped by their own success, especially by the complexity it creates in their lives. On top of this, they, like all of us, are living in a world characterized by increasingly rapid change and unpredictability. So, while they've already "made it" according to most people's definitions of success, they still want to keep growing, not just in business but also in life, and they want to increase their freedom while they do it. This is why they come to us.

Every tool and concept created at Strategic Coach comes from first principles. Dan has a special talent for being able to observe people and the obstacles to their growth (including his own) and to zero in on the root cause in their mindset. He then asks questions, provides new context, and develops simple and powerful tools and structures to help them see and transform their thinking. The laws and many of the coaching tips in this book are the product of that process, and they apply to everyone, not just entrepreneurs. Anyone can use the wisdom in this book at any stage in life. Look in any place, in any culture, in any situation, at people of any age, and you'll see that where there is growth, these laws are in action.

As an example, we also live this every day in our company culture with our team of about 120, spread over two continents. "Always be growing" is our own short form of our larger purpose statement (which you can find at the end of Law Nine), and through her leadership Babs Smith, Dan's wife and business partner, supports the whole Strategic Coach team in doing this.

Though shifts in thinking can happen very quickly, the ability to maintain a growth mindset through even the most challenging of circumstances comes with practice and awareness. The simple structure of the laws can bring you back to that mindset every time. Once you read the chapters, a glance at just the table of contents, where the ten laws are listed out, can be enough to keep you on track or help you find your way back if you feel stuck or in need of a boost. In this edition, we've added more coaching at the ends of the chapters and a new thinking tool, The Growth Focuser, at the end of the book to help you cultivate your growth mindset even more proactively.

The Laws of
LIFETIME
GROWTH

ALWAYS MAKE YOUR FUTURE
BIGGER THAN YOUR PAST

Introduction

The Desire to Grow

Growth is a fundamental desire of all human beings. No matter what kinds of goals you have or what you strive for, whatever you want to see in your life that's not there now is a sign of this desire. Growth is at the root of everything that gives us a feeling of accomplishment, satisfaction, meaning, and progress. It is making your future bigger than your past.

Yet sometimes people do stop growing. We all have images we can call to mind. The movies and literature are full of them, as is real life. Been to a school reunion lately? There are people who haven't changed much in the last 10, 15, or 20 years. Depending on where you're at, this may be comforting or shocking. You may be familiar with the retiree who's driving his wife crazy because he suddenly doesn't know what to do with himself; the addict whose life has become solely focused on whatever it takes to find the next fix; the man who is still treating women the same way he did 40 years ago and doesn't understand why they don't respond the same way; the person whose life consists of clocking in and out day after day at a dead-end job, going home, sleeping, and then doing it all over again.

There are examples all around us of people who for some reason have stopped growing, either temporarily or indefinitely. If you've picked up this book, chances are you don't want to be one of them. Maybe you're feeling a bit stuck. Maybe you're in the midst of a particularly challenging period of growth, so you're looking for insight, encouragement, or direction; or maybe you just want all the resources you can get on your side as you pursue your own growth path. Most of us struggle with issues related to growth at various points in our lives, because as much as we desire it, growth is often not easy. The entrepreneurs we work with at Strategic Coach are some of the most successful and internally motivated people on the planet, and yet they face just as many challenges in their growth as anyone else does.

In a world where technology continues to speed up change exponentially, the ability to keep growing has become a basic necessity for anyone who wants to consistently thrive. The good news is that those who master it have access to unprecedented abundance. The road to such mastery lies in cultivating a growth mindset so that you naturally choose growth more often than not in the countless opportunities that life presents us every day.

The ten laws in this book are like mirrors you can use to reflect your behavior so you can see if it's supporting or undermining your growth. Use them as you would a hallway mirror on your way out the door—do a quick check to make sure everything looks good, adjust if necessary, and then carry on. Or take a longer, more studied look to reveal areas that might take more work to transform. The laws are useful for this purpose because it's often hard to tell whether you're on the right path just by how you feel. Every once in a while, we can all use a "mindset reset" (as one of our team members calls it) when it comes to growth.

Harvard professor Rosabeth Moss Kanter has wisely observed that, "everything looks like a failure in the middle." Sometimes growing pains can feel like failure —and sometimes failure is a part of growth. Successful entrepreneurs know this well. Most of them fail before they succeed. Dan refers to his experience of going bankrupt and getting divorced on a single day in August 1978 as "market research." That doesn't mean these events felt any less like failures at the time, but instead that the lessons he took out of them were essential to building the growing multimillion-dollar company he and his life partner, Babs Smith, run today.

Checking in with the laws can help you to stay on course or renew your commitment when growth is difficult. In many of the examples in this book, challenging or seemingly less-than-ideal situations offered people rich opportunities to grow their way into much better circumstances. The laws can help you to extract the maximum value from experiences you might otherwise try to avoid or forget.

It also pays to check your behavior against the laws when things are going well. Getting what you want or achieving your goals can make you feel good, but it won't necessarily keep you on the path to further growth. In fact, it can often lead to growth traps.

Things like money, applause, rewards, comfort, and even a brilliant past can be quite seductive. If these *means* to growth begin to overshadow purpose, performance, contribution, confidence, and the sense of a bigger future—things that *drive* growth—they can quickly undermine your ability to keep growing in the future.

These laws come from our observations about what makes growth happen. If the word *law* makes you uncomfortable, try thinking about this message on a tongue-in-cheek T-shirt we saw recently in the neighborhood: It had a picture of a policeman holding up his hand, accompanied by the caption "Obey gravity! It's the law." Of course, natural laws operate whether you obey them or not. If you disregard gravity and jump off a rooftop, it won't be the "gravity police" that get you. Likewise, no "growth police" are going to come after you if you don't follow these laws. You'll just find that you probably won't grow as much.

You might want to imagine each law as being prefaced by "You will continue to grow if ...." For example, you will continue to grow if you always make your future bigger than your past. That's the way life works. You can rely on it. By understanding these principles, you can more consciously and predictably keep yourself growing, just as scientific laws help us to predict the outcomes of actions in the physical world.

Aligning your behavior with these laws gives you more control over your own future, which allows you to increase your freedom and self-determination. It also places the responsibility for your growth squarely on your own shoulders. You can choose to engage with life in this way, or not. Growth is not always easy, but its rewards are great. Life presents us with opportunities to grow almost constantly, so when you make growth a central goal, life will always appear to be full of opportunity.

As you become more growth oriented in your behavior and thinking and as you begin to experience how this impacts your life and the lives of others, it becomes increasingly clear that the rewards of maintaining a growth mindset greatly outweigh the challenges. The desire to grow is nothing less than the love of existence—a passion for being here and a deep desire to fully explore life. When you commit to aligning your actions with the principles embedded in these ten laws, you also commit to making the most of the life you've been given—all of it. And, after all, what greater gift could you possibly give to yourself, or to the world, than that?

Always Make Your Future Bigger Than Your Past

> A bigger future is essential for lifetime growth. The past is useful because it is rich with experiences that are worth thinking about in new ways—and all these valuable experiences can become raw material for creating an even bigger future. Approach your past with this attitude, and you will have an insatiable desire for even better, more enjoyable experiences. Use your past to continually create a bigger future, and you will separate yourself from situations, relationships, and activities that can trap you there.

Your future is your property. Because, by definition, it hasn't happened yet, it exists only in your mind. This means that you can choose to make it whatever you want. The act of making your future bigger than your past is the very act of growth itself: the bigger future is the vision, and growth is what makes it real. A bigger future is your own vision of what you would like to be true at some point down the road (whether it's a week or 25 years from now) that is in your estimation bigger, better, more satisfying, or more enjoyable than what's true now. It can include anything you want to see that somehow improves your present reality: greater learning, contribution, opportunities, capabilities, understanding, confidence, quality of life, compassion, or connectedness. The list goes on and on, limited only by what you can imagine. Some people's bigger futures are mostly about themselves, while others' encompass contributions to many other people and things.

Believing in a Bigger Future

Creating a future that is bigger than your past is essentially an act of imagination. However, you have to be willing to let your imagination go there. For many reasons, people often don't. Instead they imagine life either staying the same or progressing in a predictable fashion based on what others in their family or community have done. Some even wish that life would go back to the way it was at some golden point in their past, which we know is not possible in today's rapidly changing world. Either way, their history ends up dictating their vision of the future.

In order to make your future bigger than your past, you first have to want and believe that it's possible to have a bigger future, no matter what stage you're at in life or what your circumstances are. Often, this belief alone is enough to keep you growing. And often it takes a great deal of courage.

The Courage to Think Big

Take the case of Hilda, Catherine's mother. Hilda grew up in a very poor family, the third youngest of eight children. In fact, her family was so poor that her parents couldn't afford to support their children while they finished school once they reached legal working age. All of Hilda's older brothers and sisters had quit school at 16 and taken whatever jobs they could get to help earn their keep. In the 1950s, the prospects of a decent future for a girl of 16 without a high school diploma, especially coming out of such poverty, were grim. However, Hilda was a good student and, fortunately, quite headstrong. She had a burning passion to become a teacher, but of course to do this she would have to complete her education, a lofty goal considering her circumstances. So Hilda made a brave decision: she decided to leave home and go it on her own, supported by scholarships that some encouraging teachers helped her to find. At 16, her belief in herself and her bigger future was strong enough that she left her family home forever and went to live at the YWCA. She finished high school and then university, became a teacher, and taught for more than 30 years.

The world is full of stories of people who, like Hilda, grew up without a lot of resources or encouragement but nonetheless believed that a bigger future was possible. We may wonder why some people seem to rise above crushing circumstances or very modest beginnings while others get swallowed up by them. If we look closely, the answer almost always lies in how people use their past.

Every past is rich with raw material. Joe Polish is a successful and high-spirited entrepreneur who keeps reaching bigger goals in his businesses and helping more and more people along the way. Considered a brilliant marketer and interviewer by many, Joe brings an ease and sense of fun to interviewing giants of the marketing and entrepreneurial worlds for his Genius Network[†] series and various podcasts, and he consistently attracts top entrepreneurs to every coaching group and event he runs. He has a unique talent at connecting with people and getting them to open up by catching them off guard with his zany sense of humor and very real, down-to-earth presence.

What a lot of people might not realize about Joe (though he makes no secret of it) is that the turning point that led to this life of contribution and entrepreneurial success came decades ago, when he suddenly realized in one particularly crazy moment that if he didn't get out of his current circumstances, he would die. At a critical moment in his life, he chose a bigger future, even though at that point it just meant survival. Struggling with addiction, the product of a troubled youth, he left a house of other addicts to go live with his father in another city, where he began to turn his life around. Years of dealing with pain from the death of his mother when he was four years old, bullying, sexual molestation, and moving from place to place left him withdrawn, lonely and struggling to fit in as a teenager, until he discovered escape through drugs and increasingly rebellious and out-of-control behavior.

Yet even while he was doing drugs, he was also reading a lot of psychology books. He had a fascination with understanding why people behaved the way they did. Like many kids trying to protect themselves from unpredictable, threatening people and painful circumstances, he was becoming incredibly empathetic. He was also learning that he was not wired to do harm to people. What he really wanted was to help them. He just didn't know how yet. At a young age, he'd already had a lot of intense experience—a lot of past which, with much effort, would become the foundation for a unique and ultimately very rewarding future.

After moving into a trailer with his father, Joe got a sales job and found he was really good at it. A friend soon encouraged him to try the carpet cleaning business. He started reading books on marketing, which he describes as "just applied psychology," and kept deepening his understanding of human behavior. Within six months he was able to take his sales from $2,100 a month to $12,300 a month. Soon he began teaching other carpet cleaners the marketing techniques he was honing, and his career as a marketer and consultant began to take off.

One day, he ended up joining a high-profile group with a lot of famous people and saw that some of the world's leaders—billionaires, Academy Award winners, famous athletes and politicians—were very broken. He realized that though the world admired these people, in truth, they were painfully lonely, not unlike the broken people he had encountered in his past. The same was true of many top entrepreneurs: "A lot of entrepreneurs are workaholics. 'Workaholism' is the respectable addiction."

Joe's life path has given him insight into and perspective on this pain that very few people get to see. His own painful past and being witness to the pain of others became the raw material for a desire to connect people and opportunities that he's funneled into all his business endeavors. His current bigger future involves several new projects that draw on his unique combination of hard-earned skills, resources, insights, relationships, and compassion to help entrepreneurs and addicts to improve their lives and reduce suffering. Hope, which he was blessed with from childhood, helped him to always see a bigger future even amidst all the craziness and to take action to move first towards surviving, then learning, and then growing his capabilities along with his positive influence and impact on others.

Small Steps Keep You Growing

So we've seen how people can choose a bigger future when they're young and dramatically alter the trajectory of their lives. But what if you're older or in poor health, and you have many great memories and experiences behind you but perhaps only a few years left? How do you make your future bigger than your past in that case? Even if you suspect that only months, weeks, or even days remain after a fully lived life, you can still make your future bigger than your past. Growing can be as simple as making an effort to learn something that increases your perspective on the world or using the time you have left to make a new kind of contribution.

In the last years of his life, Antonio Pijuan was a spry 98-year-old Spaniard, living outside Toronto, who still had strong opinions and an appreciation of pretty women. Earlier in his life he was a farmer in Catalonia, and he experienced the Spanish Civil War and two world wars firsthand. Antonio remained intensely curious about the world despite having lived through almost a century of history. Because he was no longer as agile as he used to be, television had become his window on much of what was new and interesting. After seeing a feature on the Bata Shoe Museum in Toronto, he asked his granddaughter, Lisa, to take him there. He couldn't believe that there could be so many shoes in one building! At the end of the day, he said to her in Spanish, "Thank you. I learned so much today."

This is an example of how a bigger future doesn't have to be grand or flashy. It doesn't have to involve great leaps forward. Most growth happens as a result of many small steps. The key is to keep taking them.

Making the Most of the Future You've Got

Sometimes people's futures get cut short by events beyond their control. But a bigger future is not about how much time you have left; it's about what you do with that time. Here's where we pick up the story of Hilda again.

Hilda truly loved teaching and learning. Both were intrinsic to who she was. She knew she was making a contribution to her students' lives, and their success and appreciation were her greatest rewards. It often seemed that she learned as much from them as they did from her. Once, after going missing in a hill tribe village on a trek in Thailand, she was located sitting outside a hut surrounded by all the local children. They were teaching her words in the Lahu language, and she was teaching them words in English. Bursts of laughter had given them away.

At 59, Hilda was diagnosed with a rare, untreatable form of cancer. By the time the tumor was found, she had only a few months to live. Within moments of receiving this news, she made a decision to turn her remaining time into the most significant learning and teaching contribution of her life. She resolved to handle her situation with all the grace she could muster and to give others an example of how to deal with dying in a dignified, conscious, and thoughtful way. Her first student was a young doctor who had jumped the gun and told her the night before her official diagnosis that she didn't have cancer. Gently but clearly, she explained to him how his misinformation had affected her, and her family and friends. It was a lesson he would surely not forget.

She went on to inspire many people over the following months with her attitude and courage. Dying is a difficult subject to educate people about because most of us don't want to face it. Somehow, she managed to balance hope with pragmatism—not giving up, not being in denial, but realistically and calmly talking about the future and what might happen.

When Hilda died five months later, the funeral home had to open an additional wing to accommodate all the unexpected visitors. More than 300 people went to pay their respects and celebrate what her life had meant to them. As bravely as Hilda had lived, starting with her big decision to leave home at 16, she died even more courageously. She had been determined to squeeze every opportunity for growth out of her last few months, even though in many ways her physical quality of life had been severely diminished by the disease. No matter what your circumstances, you can always make your future bigger than your past. Use what you've learned and done as a foundation for

Where Do I Start?

● *Ask yourself a future-focused question.* If you're wondering how to think about what your bigger future might look like, try starting with a question. Here's one we like: If we were sitting here three years from today, looking back on today, what would have to have happened in that time for you to feel happy with your progress? In The Strategic Coach Program™, we call this The R-Factor Question, where *R* stands for *relationship*. In this case, it's helping you to establish your relationship with your own bigger future.

● *Set goals.* Creating goals for yourself automatically takes you out of the past and creates a bigger future. If you're having trouble coming up with meaningful goals, a good way to start is to write down five or ten of your accomplishments from the past year and then think about what would represent a further achievement in each area. If building on what you've accomplished recently doesn't excite you, think about what you love to do most that gives you energy (go back as far as you have to, to remember) and ask yourself, "How can I do more of that?"

● *Take a long view.* In Strategic Coach, we like to work with 25-year time frames when thinking about really big goals. Creating your future is, after all, a mental exercise, so you can make the time frame anything you like. We like 25 years because it offers you the freedom to imagine really big change. Committing to do something really big over 25 years doesn't seem as daunting because of the time you have to get it done, and also committing to do something *for* 25 years makes you really think about what you're committing to. If you had 25 years to develop a new capability or build something extraordinary, what would it be? What would you do now to get started?

● *Do something with Laws Two to Ten.* Law One is the definition of growth itself. You can think of it as the master law with all the other laws falling underneath it, helping you make your future bigger than your past in more specific ways. If you're having trouble with the big picture, keep reading and look for something in the subsequent laws that resonates better with you. If you've already read through the whole book, the exercise at the end will help you find a law that you'd like to focus on.

Another trick is to look back at the table of contents where you'll see all the laws. You'll notice a formula in how they're written. All the words that fall under the word "future" are things that you can focus on to keep you growing. All the words at the ends of the laws (just before the period) are potential growth traps. For instance, focusing on *future, learning, contribution, performance, gratitude*, and the other words in the middle of the laws will help you make your future bigger than your past. Focusing on the *past, experience, rewards, applause, success*, and the other words at the ends of the laws can trap you. When you look at the laws this way after you've read the book and understand them, it often happens that a word jumps out immediately that you know you want to focus on more, or that is at the root of the feeling you have of being stuck or frustrated. Read the full definition of that law again (handily on the page number listed right there), and you'll likely get some ideas about what to do.

**Law
Two**

Always Make Your Learning Greater Than Your Experience

Continual learning is essential for lifetime growth. You can have a great deal of experience and be no smarter for all the things you've done, seen, and heard. Experience alone is no guarantee of lifetime growth. But if you regularly transform your experiences into new lessons, you will make each day of your life a source of growth. The smartest people are those who can transform even the smallest events or situations into breakthroughs in thinking and action. Look at all of life as a school and every experience as a lesson, and your learning will always be greater than your experience.

Our ability to learn continually is what enables us to always have a future that's bigger than the past. There is a method to doing this. Every experience you've ever had has two parts to it: the things about the experience that *worked* and the things that *didn't work*. By *worked* we mean that those parts of the experience moved you forward, adding to your sense of capability and confidence. By *didn't work* we mean the opposite: those aspects of the experience blocked or undermined your sense of capability and confidence.

Once you identify these two aspects of every experience, you begin to become aware of new ways to maximize what worked and to bypass or eliminate what didn't. New insights, wisdom, and better, more effective ways of taking action become possible. In the process, the experience is transformed into a source of growth and gains new positive meaning.

Big Learning from a Small Experience

Even a small experience has the potential to be a source of major learning. Catherine shares this example:

> I was coming home from my father's house after a dinner. He had given me lots of wonderful leftovers to bring home, as well as my old microwave oven, which he'd borrowed, and a light fixture to try in place of a broken one in the house I had just moved into. It was late and I was tired. I looked at all the stuff in my trunk and thought that I could carry all this in one load. So I piled the fixture on top of the microwave, which was quite heavy but manageable for a short

distance, and hung two bags of food on each wrist. Standing beside my car, I was quite proud of myself. Then I realized that I still had to close the trunk.

Bringing one knee up to support the microwave, I freed the hand closest to the car to push down on the trunk lid but misjudged my ability to maneuver with the weight of the bags hanging on my wrist. The lid came down quickly with a thud and latched. Sickeningly, I realized that my finger was caught in it. As the pain began to register, I realized that I would have to drop the microwave in order to free myself. Standing on one leg, there was no elegant way to do this. The light fixture hit the ground with a crash, and broken glass sprayed everywhere. It was like a scene from an old slapstick comedy. I couldn't have choreographed it better if I were Buster Keaton. Thankfully, my key fob with its button that opens the trunk was in my pocket, or I could have been stuck there for a long time.

I managed to extricate myself, and my finger, though red and throbbing, was OK. The falling microwave had left a big white gouge in the side of my car and a hole in the front of my brand new jeans. I felt incredibly stupid—busted for doing something dumb—and I was mad at myself. What had made me think this was a good idea? Then I began to think, "OK, this is ridiculous. What is the universe trying to teach me here?" And some very wise words that I had heard from my friend Edward Brown, a Zen priest, came into my head: "Carry one thing with two hands, rather than two things with one hand." It couldn't have been more literally true. I immediately saw what was not working.

In that moment, I realized that I'd been doing things like this all my life, and that I'd actually been lucky to have evaded disaster until now, albeit narrowly a few times. A grin began to creep across my face. Time to change my habits.

Besides the damage to my car, which I couldn't bring myself to pay to have fixed, I had a blackened fingernail for a month as a constant reminder every time I was tempted to take on too much. Yet my overall feeling was one of gratitude. After all, the lesson could have come when I was driving on the highway, talking on my cell phone, and eating a Popsicle: it could have been much worse. I don't do things like that anymore. What worked about the experience was that it woke me up to a bad habit that was putting me in harm's way.

Now I try to pay more attention to doing one thing at a time and giving myself permission to take a little longer. I've learned to say no when I need to and to delegate better. I'm much less stressed, and, oddly, I actually seem to get just as much done. Not juggling so many things at once has allowed me to do a better job at what really matters and to see possibilities that I was too distracted to notice before. This very unglamorous experience, as soon as I looked at it in terms of what worked and what didn't, taught me a lesson that has helped me to improve my habits and my results.

It may have also saved my life. A couple of years later, I was driving through an intersection in that same car, looking straight ahead, though there were no cars in front of me, when just out of the corner of my eye I caught a glimpse of something large coming straight at me much too fast. Instinctively, I stepped on the gas, lurched forward, and braced myself as it crushed the back of my rear quarter panel — the one with the gouge from the microwave still in it. I was shaken but uninjured. It turned out that an elderly man with poor eyesight had run a stop sign at high speed. He didn't even see me. If I had been the least bit distracted at that moment, his huge 1970s American car, which escaped unscathed, would have t-boned my little sedan right in the drivers' side door. Immediately, I felt like I'd passed some kind of test, like the universe was saying, "Okay, we know you got the lesson. Now we'll fix your car for free (through insurance) because you don't need the reminder anymore." It was kind of perfect. Dramatic, but perfect.

The Choice to Learn

You don't get to choose all the experiences you have, but you do get to choose what to do with them. You can use them as excuses, wear them as badges of honor, make them emotional triggers for when you want to go on a good rant or have a good cry, or bury them like skeletons, which always seem to resurface later. These choices do not help you to grow. Or you can use them as raw material for learning, harnessing the emotional energy behind them to drive you to make good use of their lessons.

Sometimes, remarkable innovations can come from this kind of learning, as in the case of Mary Anne Ehlert. Mary Anne grew up with a sister who suffered from cerebral palsy. While other families went out for dinner and on vacations, Mary Anne's family stayed home and took turns looking after Marcia, who required constant care. Marcia's parents devoted their lives to her care and felt guilty that they couldn't offer their other children a more normal upbringing.

As in any family that has a child with special needs, everyone was impacted. Mary Anne decided that if her friends couldn't accept Marcia, they wouldn't be her friends. She learned how to control Marcia's seizures and helped with whatever new treatments her parents had decided to try. Mary Anne was always especially close to Marcia. She credits Marcia with having taught her to say what she felt and for teaching the whole family that "it's about more than just stuff." Her family always remained close, despite the strain, and her parents stayed together, beating the odds of an 85 percent divorce rate for parents of children with special needs.

After a 20-year career in banking, which she left when her position required her to lay off 1,500 people in two days, Mary Anne decided to become a financial advisor specializing in retirement and estate planning. In this context she asked her parents how they had provided for Marcia. She discovered their greatest fear was that her sister would be left alone if something were to happen to them. Mary Anne began to look for solutions for them and quickly realized that the need went far beyond her own family. Initially drawing on her experience in the world of financial products, she began to seek out innovative solutions that would protect her sister and restore her parents' confidence and sense of control. From her experience with Marcia, Mary Anne had a unique understanding of the kinds of things families like hers faced and where the potential dangers lay—issues that started with, but went far beyond, financial planning.

Soon, she and her team were providing the Process for Protected Tomorrows[††], which encompasses a whole array of services that address the needs of both the family and the child with disabilities on many different levels. Because of her personal experience, she is able to speak very candidly to families in this situation, cutting through the denial that is so common and providing support with genuine empathy and a depth of insight and understanding that would be difficult for someone who hadn't been in their shoes. The Process for Protected Tomorrows continues to evolve as Mary Anne and her team seek out new ways to improve the lives and prospects of the families she deals with.

While some people might have dealt with a childhood like Mary Anne's by trying to "get over it" and "move on," Mary Anne chose to use her experience to create something extraordinary. By using her understanding of what worked (the love, the devotion, and the learning that Marcia brought to their lives) and what didn't work (the stress, fear, uncertainty, and sacrifice) in her family, she was able to develop solutions to improve the experiences of other families dealing with special needs. She is making a powerful contribution where there is a great need, and in the process she has also created a unique, thriving business with limitless growth potential.

Your own experience is rich with learning opportunities that you will see if you're looking for them. Transform your experiences into lessons, and you'll never feel world-weary or disadvantaged by your past. Instead, each lesson will provide the foundation for better experiences in the future.

Where Do I Start?

● *Transform your experiences.* Focus on an experience. Try to pick a specific situation like "today's conversation with Joan" rather than a broader, less easily defined collection of events like "my relationship with Joan." You might pick one that still has an emotional impact when you think about it. There's good energy to drive transformation in those feelings. Think about what worked and what didn't work in the situation. You might want to write everything down. Then think about what you could do to create a better outcome next time, and use that learning to move ahead.

● *Change the conversation.* One way to gauge if you're focused on learning or experience is to listen to yourself talking. Are you more eager to share your experience, or to listen and learn? Do you share to be heard or to move the conversation forward? Notice how you feel around people who tell the same stories over and over. Do you talk about what happened to you, or what you learned from what happened to you? Is your experience the starting point or the ending point of the conversation? Pay attention to the stories you repeat, especially if you're simply relaying your experience. Some of those situations may be candidates for the exercise above. Once you've got the learning out of an experience, the compulsion to talk about it repeatedly generally disappears.

● *Finish this book and do the exercise at the end.* We know this is only Law Two, but it's a short book! The exercise at the end, called The Growth Focuser, will step you through mining your recent experiences for growth nuggets, but you'll need to understand all the laws to get the full benefit. This is an exercise you can do on a regular basis to develop your awareness of the choices you're making day to day and how they affect your growth. Over time, as you begin to be more conscious of your thinking and to see it in terms of the laws, you'll find yourself seizing more learning opportunities in the moment rather than repeating the same experience over and over unconsciously.

Always Make Your Contribution Bigger Than Your Reward

Increased contribution to others is essential for lifetime growth. As you become more successful, numerous rewards will come your way: greater income, praise, recognition, reputation, status, capabilities, resources, and opportunities. These are all desirable things, but they can be growth stoppers. They may tempt you to become fixated on just the rewards, rather than focus on making still greater contributions. The one way to guarantee that rewards will continually increase is to not think too much about them. Instead, continue making an even more significant contribution—by helping others to eliminate their dangers, capture their opportunities, and maximize their strengths. Greater rewards will automatically result from this, and your future will continue to be filled with increasingly rewarding ways to contribute. Always focus on creating new kinds of value for larger numbers of people, and you will ensure that your contribution is always greater than your reward.

Making a contribution for its own sake solidifies and expands your relationship with the outside world. It is through this relationship that your continual growth will be funded and supported. If you're not making a contribution to others, it's easy to get caught up in your own thoughts and go around in circles. By focusing on contributing and letting the rewards take care of themselves, you anchor yourself in the real world. Through the insight and feedback you get from others, you grow your understanding of how to create greater and greater value.

Putting Value Creation First

One of the most striking things about Mary Anne Ehlert is that, even as a top agent at one of the biggest financial-services companies in the United States, she never paid attention to how much her commission would be on any product she sold. In fact, she set up her business in such a way that she wouldn't know, so that the only factor influencing her decision about what to sell a client would be whether or not it was the best available product to meet that client's needs.

When Lisa Pijuan-Nomura, an artist and successful arts programmer in Toronto, puts on a show, she never thinks about what the take at the door is going to be or how the event will pay for itself. She focuses all her attention on trying to put on the best show and trusts that if it's good, people will come. And because she produces high quality consistently, people do come, and they tell others. She has never lost money on any show she's produced.

The way in which Lisa and Mary Anne approach rewards is not a blind leap of faith; rather, it's good business practice, and good practice in any area of life where you want to grow. When you focus on making a real contribution and allow your audience to decide how it will repay you, the rewards can often be greater than you might have imagined. Focusing on the rewards is a trap because it diverts your creative energy from what generates the rewards in the first place: the value that your audience gets from what you do.

It's the Contribution That Makes Us Grow

Most of the time, the act of making a contribution itself will be a tremendous source of growth and will produce many unforeseen rewards. In 2003, Matthew Passmore was a corporate lawyer, miserable in what he describes as a very lucrative but soul-destroying career. At lunch, he would escape to the local bookstore to look at art magazines and dream. One day, the cover of arts and culture magazine *Cabinet* caught his eye with the message "Free Land Inside (not a joke)." He opened it to read a poignant and beautiful yet tongue-in-cheek piece about how the publishers had purchased a half-acre of scrub land in the desert of New Mexico, henceforth dubbed, "Cabinetlandia." Though they were offering readers 99-year leases on magazine-sized plots (just big enough to stand on with two feet together) for a penny in a section called "Readerlandia," Matt's interest immediately went to "Artistlandia," said to be reserved for future artists' projects. Inspired, he wrote to the editors with what they later described as an "outlandish and extravagant scheme for building the Cabinet National Library" on the land. The editors were tickled and published his plans and drawings. A year later, much to their surprise, he drove out to the desert with three friends and they actually built it—the cabinet embedded in a curved wall of sandbags, earth and cement, housing every issue of *Cabinet* magazine, as well as a card catalog, a guest book, and a snack bar, which at the time consisted of a bottle of water, a pair of size 10 men's work boots (for protection from scorpions and snakes) and two cans of beer. Though venturing out to a remote and desolate tract of New Mexico desert might not be most people's idea of a holiday, for Matt and his friends, it was like a vacation—only better, because they had this fun, challenging, and possibly slightly crazy objective of realizing the vision of the library. He really wanted nothing out of it other than to do it and to contribute something to Cabinetlandia. The magazine published Matt's account and photos of the installation, and later presented its story at the venerable Tate Modern gallery in London.

Cheeky and audacious as it was, for Matt, this project was the starting point of a career as a successful and sought after full-time artist operating on a global scale. The spirit of contribution has continued to be a major factor in driving his success. Rebar Art and Design Studio, which he formed with two other artists (including one who had helped build the library) became most famous for *Park(ing)*, which involves turning a metered parking spot into a temporary public park (and paying 'rent' by feeding the meter, of course). It began in 2005 as a local guerilla art intervention in his home town of San Francisco, but as people expressed interest in doing it in other places, he and his partners decided to create a simple free how-to guide and let them do it themselves rather than charging a consulting fee. By making the model available through an open-source approach, Rebar allowed individuals and communities to make it their own and use the concept to draw attention to their particular needs and purposes. It took off like wildfire. In 2011, when Rebar stopped counting, the annual event called *Park(ing) Day* had been adopted in 162 cities in 35 countries. Nearly 1,000 parks sprung up on city streets for one day in September, surprising and delighting residents and passers-by and encouraging them to think differently about a plethora of local issues. With this success came interviews on the BBC,

NPR, and other major media outlets around the world. Matt became a sought-after speaker, and Rebar's reputation was established worldwide.

Yet he is quick to point out that none of that would have happened had they approached the project as a money-making or brand-building endeavor for Rebar as it began to take off. Artists need to make a living just like everyone else, yet they sensed that this idea needed to be presented in a pure spirit of curiosity and exploration, true to its roots, so that others could adopt and adapt it without reservation. As a result, they were able to seed a global movement that has become a vehicle for civic action, awareness raising, creativity, and fun in cities around the world.

Abundance Flows to Contributors

This brings up an interesting point: people want to align themselves with others who are making great contributions. On the other hand, people do not want to partner with, create with, or give more to those who are known for taking more than they give. In fact, the tendency is to want to balance the scales and take back from those people (or organizations). For this reason, choosing to take rather than to give, fueled by the attitude that "he who has the most wins" or by the desire to gain as much as possible, regardless of the cost to others, is a shortsighted way to live. Those who do this end up devoting a lot of energy and resources to their "defense budgets." They try to protect what they've gained and envy others who have more, rather than living with a sense of abundance, trusting that they will always have what they need.

The No-Entitlement Attitude

In order to make your contribution bigger than your reward, you have to have what we call a No-Entitlement Attitude. This means you believe that you have to make some kind of valuable contribution to others before you deserve any reward. We talk about this with our entrepreneurial clients because it's an attitude that all entrepreneurs must have. If they don't succeed in offering something that others perceive as being valuable, they won't stay in business for long. But everyone can benefit from having a No-Entitlement Attitude, not just people who run their own businesses, as Gaynor Rigby realized one day early in her career at The Strategic Coach.

Gaynor is a remarkably talented, capable, bright woman with a big heart and big dreams. She left England at 18 to come to America because she felt she could have a bigger future here. After being a nanny, first in Cincinnati and later in Toronto, she took a job at The Strategic Coach as a receptionist. The company was small then, and she had big ambitions. Reality was not living up to her expectations. She was in a bit of a funk about her life, not feeling that she was making the progress she should be, unhappy to have gained some weight, and, she admits, generally feeling sorry for herself. Why wasn't the world cooperating and helping her to achieve her dreams? Could people not see what she had to offer?

Then one day, in a workshop, she heard Dan talk about the fact that entrepreneurs know they have to create value before they expect any reward, and suddenly it dawned on her: she had been waiting around for opportunity to come to her, when what she needed to do was to go out and proactively find ways to contribute. It was a life-altering realization.

Immediately, she began to apply her considerable resolve to transforming her life. She began to eat better and exercise. She started looking around the office for systems and structures that could be improved and began initiating these improvements herself, coming up with plans, running them by Babs and Dan, and getting the OK to go ahead and make changes.

Gaynor went on to become director of sales and marketing for Strategic Coach and eventually left to become CEO of her own company back in the UK. Initially building on things she learned as a nanny about how to motivate people, she grew into a highly talented and respected leader known for her ability to take on just about anything and get it done, and then delegate or systematize the maintenance and move on to the next thing. She's happy with where her life is now and the fact that it's been created entirely on her own terms. All the rewards she wanted, and a good many that she never expected, have come as by-products of her contributions. They've allowed her to see even bigger possibilities and to seek out ways in which she can use her talents to have even more rewarding growth experiences. And she's the first to acknowledge that the day she decided to make her contribution bigger than her reward was the day she made this bigger and still-growing future possible.

Where Do I Start?

● *Practice a No-Entitlement Attitude.* When you believe that you need to create value first in order to receive any reward, you will automatically be more focused on contribution. Most of us are susceptible to thinking that we deserve things once in awhile. It's a conditioned response that has been built into our thinking because there are so many messages around us reinforcing the idea that we are entitled to things. Often, these messages come from people or organizations that want to manipulate us in some way or co-opt us into their agendas. A No-Entitlement Attitude keeps you free of these other agendas and focused on your contribution.

● *Look for ways to make a contribution.* Be like Gaynor and get creative. See where there are unmet needs that you might be able to help with. Volunteer. Go above and beyond the call of duty. Do it for its own sake and for the sake of growth. Trust that rewards will come, and be sure to recognize them when they do, in the form of new opportunities, capabilities, confidence, or other benefits you may not be expecting. Paradoxically, even not receiving rewards can be quite beneficial as it can be a quick indicator that you're working with the wrong audience or that you need to re-assess what's needed. Either can be the first step to finding a more promising path for growth if you use it as a learning opportunity (see Law 2). Entrepreneurs use this kind of feedback from the marketplace all the time to make strategic decisions.

- *Beware of "reciprocity."* It may seem like it's only fair to negotiate that for everything you give you get something in return. However, this often limits the growth potential in relationships by focusing the parties on "the deal" and who's getting what or who's getting more, rather than simply on contributing to one another. At Strategic Coach, though we're very much a for-profit business, we don't ask for or accept any financial remuneration from any of the companies we recommend, even when we bring them very significant amounts of business. This allows us to openly promote what we believe will help our clients with no question of ulterior motives and no messiness around tracking or payments or who's getting the better side of the deal. Those we promote, in turn, are appreciative that we truly value what they're offering and are open

Always Make Your Performance Greater Than Your Applause

Increased performance is essential for lifetime growth. If you become more skillful and useful, you will receive greater applause from an expanding audience. This can be intoxicating, and the temptation will be to start organizing your life around other people's recognition and praise—to keep repeating what got you the applause in the first place—rather than moving on to something new, better, and different. When this happens, the danger is that applause will become more important to you than your improved performance. The greatest performers in all fields are those who always strive to get better. No matter how much acclaim they receive, they keep working to improve their performance. Continually work to surpass everything you've done so far, and your performance will always be greater than your applause.

The future is always created through action, through performance. We can have an idea or a vision of a bigger future, but the idea and vision become real only when we take actions that are directly focused on achieving specific goals.

Applause resulting from performance is just a by-product. Obviously, it can be a very useful and valuable by-product, but it should never be the main focus. For a person to keep growing, the central focus always has to be the performance itself—never other people's response to it. To contrast this with Law Three, unlike contribution, which is about the receiver (that is, there is no contribution if the receiver doesn't perceive it as a contribution), performance is about the performer. It comes from within and is measured from within.

You have control over your performance. You never have control over other people's responses, approval, or applause. The goal here is always to be getting better; to appreciate how far you've come, but also to keep striving to go further, always making your future bigger than your past. A bigger future demands greater performance on your part. A bigger future requires that your skill and mastery keep improving.

Growing through Performing

The process of improving performance is where growth happens. In striving to better our performance, we engage our passions and talents, and search for ways to stretch them to new levels. Many of the obstacles we come up against require us to grow in ways that impact much more than our performance in any one area. But the desire for a better performance is what gives us the focus and motivation to take on and conquer these challenges.

Todor Kobakov admits, with a smile, that he was "a very arrogant 16-year-old," freshly arrived in Canada from Bulgaria, when he met his piano teacher, William Aide, at the University of Toronto's Faculty of Music. The first day he met Professor Aide, Todor told him straight out that he wasn't interested in playing the classical piano anymore. He had no plans to become a concert pianist and was instead interested in composition and jazz. Shortly after, his attitude changed, as Professor Aide quickly helped him to see how much enjoyment and possibility for new skill development there were in playing the piano.

In the first two years of study, Todor gradually learned from Professor Aide that musical performance was not just about the notes and technical skill, but that it was also, and most importantly, a personal representation of the character of the performer. He and his fellow students began to realize that what each of them was really working on was how to become a better person, not just a better pianist—that the two went hand-in-hand. In his efforts to continue improving, Todor became more conscious of qualities in his character. Through music, he discovered some things about himself that he wanted to change and also good qualities that he wanted to build on. This self-knowledge improved his ability to control his performances and to express himself through them in ways that told more unique and personal stories through the music.

When Todor and Professor Aide parted after four years, having developed a personal friendship along the way, his teacher said, "I think I've taught you how to improve yourself on your own from this point on." By his late 20s, Todor was strikingly self-possessed and articulate, with a modest wisdom that belied his age. His experience of learning how to be a better classical pianist helped him to grow into a more mature and well-rounded person during his university years. Even more important, it left him with the ability to grow continually in his life through the act of pursuing better and better performances. He says he still likes to play certain pieces every few years that he hasn't played in a long time, because the way he performs them differently now shows him how he has changed as a person.

It's about the Experience

Though Todor receives applause for his performances, it means very little to him. In fact, he says in honesty, the applause sometimes makes him sad because it means that the performance is over. His attitude is that, as a musician, you don't play with the intention of impressing the audience. Rather, what happens in a great performance is that the performer and the audience together celebrate the greatness of the music. The performer "applauds" the music through his or her performance, and the audience applauds more literally. His focus is always on the music.

This is true of other kinds of performance, too. When the performer is "onstage," he or she is focused on creating an experience that combines many elements besides just the audience's response. An audience that is paying attention will notice and appreciate the artistry that goes into orchestrating such an experience. It may not applaud literally, but these are often the kinds of performances that receive big tips, great performance reviews, letters of thanks, citations, and other kinds of recognition.

People who take pride in their performance and strive to create greater and greater experiences for their audiences can grow in any situation. It could be a fast-food order taker who is able to simultaneously, and seemingly effortlessly, ring in your order, placate your rambunctious kids, smile understandingly at you, and get everything you ordered balanced on the tray so that you can take it with your one free hand, in one seamless performance. Those kinds of everyday performances require that people be completely present and engaged in what they are doing, just as a performer is onstage. If they do it just for the enjoyment, energy, and challenge it gives them—what we often call "taking pride in one's work"—then they will keep growing. If they do it for the external recognition, then chances are they will stop growing, either because the recognition is gone once the novelty wears off or because they only have to keep doing the same thing to get the same response, and there is no internal drive to improve.

Keeping the Performance Fresh

There's a story, which may be apocryphal, that Dan likes to tell about Sir Laurence Olivier and what he allegedly did to try to keep each night's performance of a play as fresh as the opening night's. Apparently, Olivier had a ritual he would perform each night before a show. He would stand backstage, look through the peephole out into the audience, and say to himself, "This is not last night's audience. This is not last night's show. These are not last night's actors. This is not last night's play. These are not last night's lines," and so on. By doing this, he would make himself fully present for that night's performance, even though he had played the role many times before.

The true sign of a talented performer is that he or she can perform the same material over and over and make it seem different every time. Each performance is created in the moment out of the elements that are there, including the performer's state of mind, the characteristics and responsiveness of the audience, the venue, and any other factors present at the time of the performance. Therefore, each performance offers a unique learning experience to the performer and a chance to test his or her skills in this new situation. But it has to be viewed this way for the learning to occur.

Dan has this story of how he turned his attitude around to take advantage of what could have been a negative situation:

I do a lot of speaking engagements around the country. Usually, there is a minimum number of people or size of opportunity that the team will book me for. Occasionally, though, there are mishaps, and on one particular occasion I arrived expecting to speak to 300 people, and only 30 were in attendance.

Usually, I get a lot of energy from bigger audiences, so initially this was a bit of a disappointment. But then I started thinking about it in terms of a performance. I decided that what would make this opportunity really worthwhile for me and a better experience for the audience, too, would be if I could just go out there and give the performance of a lifetime and not think about the size of the audience: just focus on giving them the best possible experience. So I went out and gave my speech with that attitude, and I got a standing ovation—and increased my abilities that day.

As a means of facilitating growth, applause can be wonderfully useful. It opens doors to all kinds of opportunities, resources, and capabilities that can support performance at an even higher level. But as an end in itself, applause becomes a growth stopper. It stifles the imagination and undermines motivation. By always focusing on improving your performance and treating applause as a by-product that you accept with gratitude, you can ensure continued growth.

Where Do I Start?

● *Create your own standards.* Athletes have the advantage of having their performance measured, both in training and in competition, so they have a clear idea of what their personal best is. Canadian Olympian speed skater Clara Hughes described skating a personal best time in her home country during the Vancouver Olympics as "the race of my life," despite the fact that on that day her time won her a bronze medal whereas she had won gold at the Turin games previously. By creating your own standards for your performance and tracking them yourself, you can celebrate your wins and measure your progress on your own terms, which helps you resist putting too much focus on external standards or recognition.

● *Separate performance from contribution.* Something that often creates confusion around this law is the use of the word "performance" in the workplace as in "performance review" in a way that makes it difficult to distinguish from contribution. A performance review is generally a measurement of your performance against external standards, like the requirements of your job, which are really your contribution in the form of results you create for your team or company. Here, we are differentiating performance to separate out how you go about getting those results (performance), which is entirely up to you, from the contribution those results make, which is judged by others. Many people find that they can keep doing the same thing over and over and make a valuable contribution because those results are needed. However, if you start to feel that your work is getting boring or stagnant, it may be time to look at the Laurence Olivier story at the beginning of this chapter and think about how you can keep your performance fresh and exciting by shifting your mindset.

- *Treat applause as something to be grateful for, not an entitlement.* Being grateful for applause insulates you from the temptation to start expecting recognition. When part of you is focused on expecting applause, that same part of you is not available to contribute to your performance.

- *Try to just be present in the moment.* One thing that can undermine performance is having part of your mind thinking about the end of the performance and the applause it brings before you're actually there. In order to perform at your best, you need to have all your focus in the moment. If you do this, applause will take care of itself.

Always Make Your Gratitude Greater Than Your Success

Increased gratitude is essential for lifetime growth. Only a small percentage of people are continually successful over the long run. These outstanding few recognize that every success comes through the assistance of many other people—and they are continually grateful for this support. Conversely, many people whose success stops at some point are in that position because they have cut themselves off from everyone who has helped them. They view themselves as the sole source of their achievements. As they become more self-centered and isolated, they lose their creativity and ability to succeed. Continually acknowledge others' contributions, and you will automatically create room in your mind and in the world for much greater success. You will be motivated to achieve even more for those who have helped you. Focus on appreciating and thanking others, and the conditions will always grow to support your increasing success.

Everyone has his or her own idea of what success means. Some people measure success by what they have in their lives, which may include material possessions or circumstances, and also more esoteric things—qualities like love, wisdom, and life skills; particular accomplishments; certain kinds of relationships; and a particular quality of life. The trouble is, it's possible to attain all these things and still not be happy. Usually, this happens when people reach their idea of success, think they've "arrived," and stop growing. When the enjoyment and energy created by the growth process itself subside, there's a hole, despite all the trappings of success. For the person committed to lifetime growth, success is a process, not a destination. Living a successful life becomes a matter of constantly growing. Gratitude makes constant growth a given.

Appreciating What Makes It All Possible

Gratitude is the greatest guarantee of continual successful interaction with the world over an entire lifetime. This is because all of our accomplishments and capabilities are made possible by the talents and contributions of others. Just look around you right now if you need proof. Look at everything in your environment that was created by others: the tools you use, the food you ate earlier, the furniture you're sitting on, the paper this book was printed on. It's almost inconceivable how many people, how much ingenuity, and how much effort were required to create the situation you're in right now. No success happens without the right combination of elements and circumstances aligning, whether you believe it's by luck, fate, design, or destiny.

Practicing "Proactive Gratitude"

We are taught to thank someone when he or she does something for us, but there is much more in the world to be grateful for. We can be "proactively" grateful by appreciating more about the world we live in—the people we know and don't know, everything that creates the environment in which we are able to grow and live productive lives. What we appreciate appreciates. We see the value in people and things through proactive gratitude. Once we see this value, we naturally treat these people and things with greater respect. People want to work with people who appreciate them. Resources are drawn to where they are valued most. The world responds to gratitude by making more of everything we appreciate available to us.

It took years for Dan to convince Tony and Mary Miller that the way to address the industrywide problem with staff turnover affecting their successful janitorial business was to give the cleaners more time off. It seemed so counterintuitive and went completely against how things were done. Yet finally Tony relented and tried an experiment, giving them an unprecedented three weeks off. Immediately, things began to change. The turnover rate of 300 percent declined dramatically. People stayed, and as they stayed longer, they got better at working in teams and started to produce better results in shorter times. It was then that Tony and Mary knew they were on to something. They realized that by appreciating and responding to the broader needs of their workers, who were almost exclusively new immigrants, they could transform the nature of their business and do some good in the world, too.

New immigrants don't get as much real time off as other people do. Their challenges with the language barrier and with having to figure out how things work differently in their new country mean that once the necessities of life are taken care of, there often isn't much time left for leisure. Giving employees more free time was a way of proactively acknowledging this difficulty and saying, "We appreciate your challenges and the courage you're demonstrating by starting a new life in a new country." This is proactive gratitude: it does not say "Thank you because you've done something for us," but rather expresses the broader message, "We're grateful that there are people who want to be cleaners, and we appreciate these immigrants' value as people with courage and hopes and dreams for a better future."

Tony and Mary began offering English lessons and then created a program that would allow cleaners to eventually buy their own homes. These kinds of benefits were unheard of in the industry. Though the Millers had no guarantee that what they were doing would generate better results or that the cleaners would respond, they took a chance and did it anyway—and their staff did respond. Many started referring their relatives. Turnover continued to drop and productivity continued to improve. Word spread among the immigrant community of this company that treated its employees like people with dreams and futures and not like disposable labor.

Soon Tony and Mary's problem became the difficulty of explaining how they were able to legitimately price their services so well as they underbid competitors for contracts. It was hard for prospective clients to understand how the Millers' team could be so much more efficient than those of other cleaning companies. The answer, in a nutshell, was appreciation of their employees, which allowed them to create a process for cleaning buildings that no other company could compete with. Not only did it transform the lives of their cleaners, but it also transformed Tony and Mary's understanding of how to approach business and blew wide open their perceptions of what was possible, allowing them to envision a much bigger future.

Here's a quick exercise to try that proves how gratitude can change your outlook. Pick any person you know, and ask yourself, "What do I appreciate about this person?" Write down everything you can think of. Try to come up with at least ten things. Get creative if necessary. Then observe how your attitude toward that person has changed. If you want to take it a step further, let the person know what you're grateful for, and see what his or her reaction is.

Pablo Neruda once wrote a book of poetry called *Odes to Common Things*. Reading through the poems—about a salt shaker, a chair, a can opener—gives one a completely new sense of how even the most ordinary objects play meaningful roles in our lives. We can find this meaning if we look for it; and in the process we grow, and we increase our connection to those things. The same is true of people.

Connectedness, Commitment, and Humility

The more successful you become, the more important it is to practice proactive gratitude. With gratitude come three prime ingredients for lifetime growth: connectedness, in that you see yourself as part of something larger; commitment, in that you want to contribute to that larger reality because you see the value of the contributions that other people and things are making; and humility, in that you see yourself as a unique part of the world around you, but not the most important part. When you're connected, committed, and humble, there's always more to learn, and you're open to learn from anything and anyone who might have something to teach you.

Gratitude, by its very nature, also automatically works to eliminate three mental characteristics that most undermine individual success in an interactive world: isolation, egotism, and arrogance. People who isolate themselves are cut off from crucial knowledge, resources, and capabilities that others can provide. People who are egotistical continually destroy the goodwill and support of others. And people who are arrogant increase the opposition and hostility of other people. By cultivating gratitude, we can immunize ourselves against all three of these threats to growth and continued success.

Where Do I Start?

● *Write down what you're grateful for.* A common, and always effective, way to focus your attitude on gratitude is to write down five or ten things you're grateful for every day. You can practice proactive, creative gratitude when you do this and include people, events, and circumstances you just appreciate for their own sake, as well as those that have directly benefited you in some way.

● *Express your gratitude!* The late Dan Taylor, a highly successful entrepreneur and longtime client and coach in The Strategic Coach Program, ended every meeting and every encounter with our team by expressing his gratitude for the opportunity in a heartfelt way. As a result, people loved working with him and always felt appreciated and valued in the process. Expressed gratitude almost always has a ripple effect.

● *Make it about them.* People like to be appreciated in different ways. If you're appreciating a particular individual, doing it in a way that's meaningful to that person will always land better. Some people prefer not to have attention drawn to themselves and may prefer a more private form of appreciation, like a thank-you card or a gesture or gift that has particular meaning to them. Others enjoy more public recognition. If you don't know someone well enough to know how to best appreciate that person, you can ask someone who does. Often an assistant or a friend will know what the person likes and how they might appreciate being thanked. For one person it might be a nice bottle of wine; for another, a donation to a favorite charity—in their name if they like recognition, or anonymously if they're the type who likes to keep things more private. You get the idea.

**Law
Six**

Always Make Your Enjoyment Greater Than Your Effort

Enjoyment is essential for lifetime growth. Some people believe that success has to be hard earned to be real. They are highly suspicious of any gains that come as a result of enjoyment. If they earn rewards this way inadvertently, they feel guilty. If others appear to be profiting from enjoyment, they question those people's morality, certain that such gains can only be ill-gotten. Meanwhile, they continue to toil away at things that give them no pleasure, suppressing any hints of enjoyment that may creep through, lest these be interpreted as signs that they're not "serious" or "professional" and deserving of success. In the process, they cut themselves off from a major source of energy, creativity, and motivation. Finding ways to get more and more enjoyment from your activities is one way to ensure continued growth. Creativity in all fields of activity is intimately linked to playfulness—the

constant desire to do new things just for the fun of it.
Approach everything you do with this sense of play,
and you will ensure that, even though you still get
as good or better results, your enjoyment is always
greater than your effort.

In the bureaucratic world, people get paid for putting in
time and effort. But entrepreneurs, who get paid only for
how much value they create, regardless of what it took to
get there, know that it's not how much time and effort you
put in that counts—what matters is the result. If you can
get the same or better result and have fun doing it, there's
nothing wrong with that. With a little ingenuity and the
right attitude, you can find ways to get enjoyment—and
growth—out of even the most daunting tasks.

Seeking Enjoyment, Finding Growth

Clifford Shearing was a mere 17 years old, working on
a lovely farm in South Africa during apartheid. The
farm had all its workers organized into teams, and
Clifford was the manager of one of them, though he
admits that he knew the least about what they were
doing—he was their manager not because of his knowledge but because he was white. To get the most out of
his workers, the farmer would assign task work every
Friday and say, "As soon as you're done, you can have

the rest of the weekend off." The tasks would always be bigger than what could be finished on a Friday, so they would encroach on the team's weekend.

One Friday, he gave Clifford's team the task of emptying a large wetland, a job that would take the entire weekend. Fed up and feeling mischievous, Clifford decided to have some fun and teach the farmer a little lesson. First, he arranged that his team would get up at 2 a.m. Then he managed to corral others from nearby farms who weren't working at that time to come help. They all set out in the dead of night, quietly rolling tractors and Land Rovers down to the site, and by 6 a.m. it was clear that they would have the whole job done by 8 a.m. Thinking this worthy of a celebration, a member of the team drove to the local butcher and bought a lamb, and everyone who had helped gathered outside Clifford's little cottage for a breakfast barbecue (or a *braai*, as they say in South Africa).

At about 9 a.m., the farmer came by and saw his entire workforce laughing, joking, and not working, although (he thought) they still had his task to complete. He immediately identified Clifford as the culprit and began berating him:

"This is typical of you, Clifford! You're undermining discipline on the farm!" And on and on. Somehow, in the midst of this barrage and in spite of his youth and the fact that he suffered from a speech impediment, Clifford managed to speak out perfectly calmly and clearly, "I don't know why you're getting so excited. We finished your silly little job a long time ago."

At this, the whole staff burst out with a roar of laughter. The farmer, his authority and status now completely undermined, said, "That's it! I've had absolutely enough of you! You have to leave this farm within two hours, and don't think you'll ever get another job on a farm in this district or anywhere else!"

Growth Sets the Stage for a Bigger Future

So Clifford packed his bags and found himself standing at the side of the dirt road outside the farm, waiting for a bus, and in that moment he had a revelation that shaped his whole life from that point on: He realized that the power of apartheid didn't rest in the government or the police or the army; it lay with all these people—the farmers and everyone else—who were really the instruments of apartheid. It dawned on him that if power was everywhere, then everyone had an opportunity to shape their world.

Clifford went on to become a globally respected scholar with a specialized interest in security issues. Decades after the incident at the farm, the understanding he had gained by pursuing questions that had arisen that day would play a key role in creating the conditions that allowed for South Africa's first democratic election, in 1994, to take place peacefully. The task force he was a part of came up with a way, based on his experience and investigations, to have those demonstrating during the elections take responsibility for keeping their own demonstrations peaceful. As a result, there was very little need for the riot police, which meant that brutal clashes that could have been fatal to the country's fledgling efforts to create democracy were avoided.

Had Clifford just grudgingly gone about his task, it is likely that his life would have taken a very different course and he wouldn't have arrived at that point to make that contribution. So, though Clifford lost his job on the farm, he gained a vision and a set of questions that have led him to a lifetime of discovery and contribution.

The Game That Engages You

Finding a way to bring enjoyment to work engages our creativity and gives us the sense that we are in control rather than being oppressed by a task. This opens us up to making new discoveries about ourselves, and perhaps, as in this case, to finding courage and strength of character we didn't know we had. If you approach life as a game with growth as the objective, you'll put yourself in the right frame of mind to engage in and enjoy the adventure, whatever it brings.

You never know what will happen when you make your enjoyment greater than your effort. A spirit of fun can bring out remarkable qualities and also inspire others in ways that are difficult to foresee. Approaching anything you want to accomplish with this attitude definitely makes it easier to bring others on board to help. Making something fun encourages others to engage with it and to want to be a part of it.

Chad Johnson, an entrepreneur from Oregon, is a master at this. As a kid, he was always making up games and challenges for his many siblings and cousins to keep them entertained and learning. He even started his own circus when he was nine, with the kids as performers and the local adults as the audience. With his wife and their own 11 children, cleanup after meals could be a huge job, so Chad turned it into a game. They call it SCAMP for "Speedy Clean After Meal Party" and the goal is to completely restore order and cleanliness in 15 minutes. Since Chad used to be a firefighter, there are always a few paramilitary elements in his games these days. For SCAMP, a different kid gets to be the leader each time. They all fall in and do a team cheer, then the timer goes, they turn on music, and everyone starts doing their thing. Everyone has pre-assigned responsibilities and nobody's done until everyone's done. If you don't pull your weight, the "team" can give you extra jobs, and the bigger kids help the smaller ones to make sure they get done in time. As a result, not only is cleanup relatively stress-free and fun, the kids also learn leadership, responsibility, and teamwork.

Your Unique Ability Will Help You to Grow

There is another important reason to seek enjoyment over effort: the things we are best at and most passionate about, that offer us the best opportunities for never-ending improvement and growth, are activities that bring us enjoyment. At Strategic Coach, we call these your Unique Ability activities. Every person has a Unique Ability, and the best opportunity to make a contribution comes from discovering it and finding ways to create greater and greater value with it in the world.

Often people get trapped doing what they are very good at but not passionate about. Though these efforts may bring rewards, they do not bring enjoyment or significant growth over the long term. People may get marginally better at activities for which they have no passion, but they will never be motivated to grow in these areas the way they are when they do the things they truly love to do. So if you're focused on activities that bring you no enjoyment, chances are it's at the expense of doing what would offer you the greatest opportunities for productive growth—what would allow you to truly make a unique contribution if you focused on it.

We see this often with entrepreneurs who trap themselves in managing their teams and handling details that would be much better left to others instead of strengthening client relationships, selling, or coming up with innovative solutions—whatever they do that really charges them up and creates their best results. It's easy to convince yourself that these other tasks are necessary, and sometimes they are, but do you really have to do them yourself? Sometimes the answer is yes, but often, with a little honesty and a little creativity, they can be delegated, done differently, or eliminated altogether. So if you're finding that your effort is greater than your enjoyment, it may be a sign that you're doing something you'd be better off not doing.

Do what you love and find ways to inject fun into what you do, and you will open up opportunities for ongoing growth that you didn't know existed.

Where Do I Start?

● *Use measurement and challenges to turn tasks into games.* We like to use a technique we call "sprints" to break down large tasks into manageable chunks and turn them into a game. The idea with a sprint is to set a measurable goal and then challenge yourself to finish it within a certain time. For Dan, this might mean writing a page in 20 minutes. If he finishes in 10, he's ahead of the game. Keep track of your results and, if you like, give yourself a prize for achieving your goal. As you challenge yourself like this, you not only make it more fun to do tasks that might otherwise seem repetitive or daunting, but you also create an impetus to find better ways of doing things. Try to set up a game you can win that still stretches you a bit. This helps you to get the task done and grow while doing it.

● *Innovate more enjoyable ways to get the desired result.* This has a lot to do with attitude. If you start with the idea that something could be enjoyable rather than drudgery, you can build enjoyment right into it. Chad Johnson's SCAMP game is an example of this. Ask yourself, what can I do to make this more fun? If you're short on ideas, enlisting the help of others through an online community like Quora or Facebook, or just asking around the old fashioned way may turn up suggestions you can work with.

● *Give yourself permission to use "enjoyment level" as a filter.* We often see people reluctant to give up doing things they don't like because they either hold the mindset that "doing things you don't like is just a part of life" or that "it's not fair to give this crappy job to someone else." Here's a different perspective: One thing we've learned in our work with Unique Ability is that, because everyone has a Unique Ability, and everyone's is different (hence "unique"), what you dislike is inevitably someone else's passion—so by hanging onto it you're actually depriving someone else of doing what they love! The trick is to find that person. Busy entrepreneurs who can't stand organizing are often surprised to find that there are people out there who would relish the opportunity to create order out of their chaos. If you're interested in discovering your own Unique Ability and learning about tools that can help you identify others who enjoy doing what you don't, visit lifetimegrowth.com, strategiccoach.com, or amazon.com and look for *Unique Ability 2.0:*

Discovery, our comprehensive book and workbook that will guide you through the process we've been using to help our clients discover theirs for more than 15 years.

● ***Recognize that you can have fun and still be taken seriously.*** At Strategic Coach, we have a lot of clients and team members who are both really good at what they do and really fun to be around. If people criticize you for having too much fun when you're doing your job, or think that you must not be working hard enough because you seem to be enjoying yourself too much, it might be time to seriously consider whether that's an environment you want to stay in. In workplaces that truly foster and appreciate growth, seeing people enjoying their jobs is the norm, not the exception.

Always Make Your Cooperation Greater Than Your Status

Cooperation is essential for lifetime growth. When people come together around a common purpose, they can achieve results that no individual could accomplish alone. Working with others and creating opportunities for increased cooperation makes greater things possible in our lives and in the world. Yet some people mistakenly assume that if they work with others or treat coworkers as equally valuable contributors, people will somehow think less of them, or it will diminish or obscure the value of their own contribution. These people's attachment to their status keeps them from cooperating with others and puts a ceiling on their growth. Always make your cooperation greater than your status, and you will find unlimited possibilities and synergies in combining your talents and opportunities with those of others.

Some people are born with status—members of royal families, children of celebrities, members of higher classes in social environments where class structures are still observed. For most people, though, status comes as your contributions and achievements grow, and you are recognized for them. While there's nothing wrong with being recognized, if your primary goal becomes achieving or preserving a level of status, you will cut yourself off from an important source of more wide-ranging achievement and growth: cooperation with others.

Focusing the Contributions of Others

Cooperating and facilitating cooperation do not mean you have to go along with what others say or merely respond to their needs. Cooperation is about focusing on a common objective and allowing everyone to make his or her best contribution. When people put their need for status ahead of the desire for cooperation, their personal agendas become obstacles to progress. The act of preserving status involves never appearing to be wrong, always taking credit, and always preserving the appearance of superiority over others. This takes up a lot of energy. It also gets in the way of achieving breakthrough results.

Trading Status for Results

One arena where you see a lot of people protecting and increasing their status is politics. After all, politics is about power, and status generally gives a person power. Politicians rely on their status in the eyes of the public to get elected, and they use their status in the eyes of other power brokers to get things done. That's why Ruth Samuelson stood out so much in her approach to the office of county commissioner in Mecklenburg County, North Carolina. Ruth got into politics to create results, and she quickly began to see that the way to achieve that was to get to know people, especially the people most likely to oppose her. She started doing this even before announcing that she would run for office. Ruth met with all the influential people who might oppose her candidacy and asked them questions like, "What dangers do you feel are facing the people of Mecklenburg County?" "What opportunities do you see us having available to us as a community?" and "What concerns do you have about my running for office?" This gave her potential opponents an opportunity to feel that they were being heard and also to realize that Ruth was like-minded on many important issues. In the end, they couldn't find anyone to run against her.

Cooperation Begins with Conversation

Later, when she was in office and tough issues came up, she was able to accomplish results by getting people to cooperate, even if they were from different parties or had different interests, because she was known as someone who would listen and cooperate. She was the one who was willing to say, "All right, what is it that you need out of this, and how can I get what you need *and* what I need so that we both end up with a better objective than if we fight each other on it?" Ruth understands that cooperation begins with conversation: asking intelligent and open-ended questions; listening; respecting others' opinions; and understanding people's real concerns, as well as what opportunities they're most excited about and what strengths they have to contribute. With this information in hand, she is able to find common ground for communication and agreement that other politicians miss.

Some of the most effective work Ruth has done has been completely out of the limelight. Quietly, she finds creative ways to allow people to put their egos and political affiliations aside so that they can cooperate to create the best results for constituents. This often has to be done behind the scenes. For example, without fanfare, she managed to help orchestrate the move of a $160 million courthouse, an initiative that saved taxpayers tens of millions of dollars, by cooperating with people from the opposing party as well as county government and staff. For primarily aesthetic reasons, the courthouse was to be built in a location that would require the destruction and relocation of several other structures. In the new location, the county will be able to erect a much better building for significantly less money and with many fewer complications.

Why had no one else seen this better solution? They hadn't asked the questions Ruth asked. When she realized what was going on, she immediately went into action to bring together the parties that needed to cooperate in order to craft the solution. Had it been done publicly, politics would have entered into the picture to a much greater extent, and the cooperation between the various parties and officials would not have been possible. Because people were able to put aside status-related issues and just work together to accomplish what needed to be done, a potential political mess was avoided with relative efficiency.

Ruth's unique approach has earned her a rare degree of trust from all sides and a reputation for being committed to finding the best solution for the public. Her creativity in fostering cooperation where none seemed possible and the results she has been able to obtain for the people of Mecklenburg County have grown her confidence about what she can make happen. Her latest project is a PBS special on the history of African Americans in Charlotte, North Carolina, for which she raised funding to help reduce local racial tension. Again, the project is based on the idea that mutual understanding leads to increased cooperation.

She decided to take her name off of all the funding materials because her political affiliation was drawing resistance from leaders in the opposing party. Making her cooperation greater than her status is a habit that gives Ruth powers of persuasion and a kind of effectiveness that constantly draws opportunities her way.

The Cooperation Bypass

People who get great results through increasing cooperation are often perceived as a threat by those who are concerned with preserving status. If you're focused on status, consciously or unconsciously, it's very difficult to even understand how people who work more cooperatively get their results. You risk being bypassed or blindsided by people who come from out of nowhere and grow right past you, stealing your accolades along the way. The annoying thing is, that's not even the part they care about. They're just in it for the growth.

Jonathan B. Smith is one of those bypassers. Like Ruth, he gets energy from creating results, and he loves to learn in the process. Jonathan was raising money for the Leukemia and Lymphoma Society through a program that allowed the fund-raisers to go on a trip if they raised a certain amount. It was suggested that he send letters to solicit donations and then follow up with phone calls. Statistically, only about one in four letters sent in a fund-raising campaign results in a donation.

Jonathan owns a company that specializes in Internet marketing for Web sites, and he loves to find ways to use online tools to solve problems. He immediately saw that having a Web site for fund-raising could bring in more donations than a letter-writing campaign because people could just give their money online on the spot rather than having to send in a check, which they often forget to do after getting off the phone.

He decided to test his theory just for fun and try to raise enough money through a Web site that he could go on the trip. So he built the site, and then began calling his friends and asking if they would donate money. But this approach was limited to his direct sphere of influence—the people he knew and could call. Once he decided that he'd raised enough money from his friends and family, he applied his knowledge of search engine marketing to the site so that other people on the Internet who were looking to make donations could find it easily.

Immediately it started working. Donations flowed in from strangers. And so did questions and comments about the Leukemia and Lymphoma Society site, and what people were looking for on it. Jonathan's site had inadvertently become a hub for people who wanted to donate to the Leukemia and Lymphoma Society in the easiest possible way. He had facilitated that process for them and opened a valuable dialogue.

Through their questions he began to see what was most important to donors, and he modified his site to meet their needs. One of the first things to go was the picture of him. People didn't care about who Jonathan was. What they wanted to know was, "What's the address for the Leukemia and Lymphoma Society? Because I have my checkbook out, and I want to make a donation now." So Jonathan put this information on the site, but he also made it easier for them to donate directly online. He found answers to their other questions, too, like how to get acknowledged for a donation, how to donate a car or boat, where to donate hair. All of this information found a place on the site, but making donations, the number one concern, stayed front and center.

Through this cooperation with would-be donors, he created a highly effective online fund-raising vehicle. This caused some people at the Leukemia and Lymphoma Society's national headquarters to question his motives. Though all the funds went to them, they wanted to know why he was spending his own money and time to raise money for the society, and why he should be allowed to have his own site. They were particularly perturbed that his site was disrupting the traditional system of state-based fund-raising territories, as it drew donations from all across the country with no regard to the donors' locations.

Jonathan's site and its success also posed a threat to the status of the society's paid fund-raisers, whose job it was to raise "major gifts"—donations in excess of $10,000. They couldn't believe that someone with no infrastructure could get a $50,000 donation in Michigan from a donor in Texas that they had been unable to bring in through traditional channels. The key in this particular case was that the donor had wanted to make the gift on December 29 and have the tax receipt issued for the same year. Doing it online through Jonathan's site allowed him to be sure that it was taken care of in time.

In all fairness to the Leukemia and Lymphoma Society, most bureaucratic structures impede cooperation at some level because they entrench hierarchy and the need to preserve status.

Status as a Product of Results

After raising $300,000 for the Leukemia and Lymphoma Society, Jonathan was named its National Man of the Year in 2004 and given its Chairman's Citation, which is normally reserved for scientists and researchers who have made notable contributions. The recognition was nice, but it's not what was important to him. More exciting to Jonathan was how powerful the Internet proved to be as a tool for facilitating cooperation among people who may not have even known the other existed until they did an online search. Diagnosed with diabetes in August 2004, Jonathan made a deal with his doctor to create a similar Web site to raise money for diabetes. This time he worked out the politics up front so that he can focus all his attention on creating results just by doing what he does best—using the

Internet to make it easy for people to solve their problems and have their needs met.

It is said that you can accomplish anything in the world as long as you don't care who gets the credit. If you let status be a by-product of the results you create through increasing cooperation, you'll keep the path open for your continued growth.

Where Do I Start?

- *Be honest about your motives.* Why are you really doing what you're doing? Is it about you and your own advancement, or is it about creating a result that benefits others? Which are you more committed to? What does your behavior say? Sometimes we can surprise ourselves with the answers to these questions. If your ego or your need for status is getting in the way of creating the best result for others, be aware that this leaves you standing still, just waiting to be bypassed by someone who is fully committed just to getting the result. If you really are committed to the result but you still feel defensive about your status, take a look at what this is costing you in terms of time, energy and resources. How big is your "defense budget"? If you were to redirect these resources towards a more cooperative approach could you get results that would speak for themselves?

- *Appreciate and invite the talents and contributions of others.* We mean this both in the sense of proactive gratitude—appreciating that there are others who can contribute and that their contributions will make for a better result—and in the sense of a plain old, much-appreciated "Thank you" for what they've done. No one wants to cooperate with people who are out to take all the credit for their efforts. If you're creating a solution for a person or group of people, like Jonathan with the donors, or Ruth with the constituents in her county, be sure to recognize that they will have a very important contribution to make. Ask them questions and be open to hearing their answers. The greater the collaboration between the people with the problem and the people who are trying to create the solution, the more effective the solution will be. Effective solutions are what elevate people's status—at least enough that they are given the opportunity to create more.

● ***Aim to be in charge rather than to be in control.*** The most powerful and effective leadership is about being in charge, not in control. What's the difference? Being in charge involves clearly communicating vision and goals and supporting your team to get the desired result. Being in control presumes that you need to personally drive every part of the process and dictate how things get done. If you believe that you have to be in control of everything, you'll stifle creativity, confidence and cooperation among team members that naturally happens when you allow talented people to figure out the best way to accomplish a common goal. There are some good books on "servant leadership" that provide guidance on how to be this kind of leader. See lifetimegrowth.com for some suggestions.

Always Make Your Confidence Greater Than Your Comfort

Increased confidence is crucial for lifetime growth. Many successful people start off life as dreamers and risk takers, but the moment they become successful, they begin to seek greater security and comfort over everything else. This attitude puts them to sleep motivationally, and they lose the confidence that made them so successful. Security and comfort are desirable by-products of goal achievement, but when they become the goal itself, they quickly stop lifetime growth. Treat any increase of comfort in your life as only a temporary stage for establishing bigger goals. Continually strive for higher goals and achievement, and your confidence will always be greater than your comfort.

All growth requires that we stretch beyond where we've been before. As we do this, our confidence about being able to take on new challenges increases. Our commitment to pursue new levels of confidence gives us the courage to overcome fear and stay in motion, continually realizing our bigger future.

Short Breaks Build Confidence

Growing confidence also requires that we periodically take "comfort breaks." These are periods of rest, which are necessary so that we can acknowledge and celebrate our achievements and rejuvenate for the next challenge—key preparation for approaching a new task with confidence. We need to take the time to say to ourselves, "I've done this and proved I can do it. Now what else does this make possible?"

Continued growth requires a balance between stretching ourselves beyond where we're comfortable, to increase our confidence to new levels, and taking comfort breaks at those new levels so that they can begin to feel normal.

It's a lot like exercising our muscles: If we constantly push our limits without any rest, we run the strong risk of burnout, injury, or at least hitting a point of diminishing returns, where more effort returns less and less progress. But if we stop for too long, we lose strength and momentum and can even lose the ability we've gained. The trick is to keep comfort breaks short enough that we don't lose our momentum; otherwise, confidence can begin to slip away, and it can be hard to get going again. We can become trapped in comfort, at which point it becomes a growth stopper.

Transforming Fear into Action

The biggest challenge to leaving our comfort zone is always fear: fear that we'll fail, fear that someone will discover that we're not as good as they thought we were, fear that we'll lose something important, fear that people won't understand what we're doing—the list goes on and on. Courage is the ability to transform these fears into focused thinking and action. New levels of capability are the reward for persisting courageously even when it feels uncomfortable or discouraging, and with these new capabilities come increased confidence. If you admire someone with greater confidence in some area, or imagine yourself there in the future, the way to get there is by leaving comfort behind and making a commitment to courageously face whatever it takes to build that capability.

Even highly successful people still experience fear often when they're reaching for a new capability, though eventually they learn to not be stopped by it. For some, it just means that the challenge is big enough and meaningful enough to be worthwhile.

Dan Taylor, whom you may remember from the fifth chapter, believed in taking on big challenges to increase his confidence. In this spirit, he wanted to do something special with his team to celebrate his 50th birthday, in October 2002. He and his team decided to create five events, to be done over the five weeks before his birthday. They included running a 26-mile stretch of Class IV and V rapids in the Gauley River, in a four-person raft with a guide; going on a 100-mile bike ride; running the Chicago Marathon; walking 50 miles in one day; and swimming 5 miles. None of the team had any cycling, whitewater-rafting, or long-distance-swimming experience. The most any of them could run was 3 to 5 miles at a time, but in five months they were going to run a marathon: 26 miles. It seemed like a suitable challenge.

Now, you might ask, why would anyone in his right mind—especially someone who doesn't have a lot of spare time because he's running a business, coaching, and creating new teaching programs on the side—want to take on something that would require so much work and preparation just to celebrate a birthday? The answer is that Dan got tremendous energy from challenges. It was important to him at this point in his life to see if he could do these things. And once the idea was in his head, it became normal to talk about it. Together, he and the team mapped out a five-month training plan that had them gradually increase their abilities in running, swimming, and cycling.

Making your confidence greater than your comfort requires that you take on new challenges despite any fears you may have. Each time you succeed, you'll create a new sense of what's normal for you that provides a new platform for growth and achievement. Think of it as building a set of stairs. Big achievements that might have seemed impossible to reach several steps ago become attainable as we build our confidence to higher and higher levels.

Come October, after much training, Dan pushed himself to the limit, physically and emotionally. He completed all the events but one: his swim was cut from 5 miles to 3 by six-foot swells and a small-craft advisory. He describes the whitewater event as "sheer terror," yet he got through it. Week after week, event after event—being alone with himself on the bike, swimming against big waves, walking 50 miles, and running the marathon—he took his belief about his physical and mental capabilities to new levels.

Dan's new normal fitness regime, after this experience, included running 22 to 30 miles a week, biking 50 to 100 miles a week, swimming for 2 hours a week, and strength training. This gave him tremendous confidence about his ongoing physical quality of life as he continued to pursue his other goals. Two other members of his team, neither of whom had run a marathon before, completed the Chicago Marathon and the river rafting, and acted as spotters on Dan's swim. One of these two went on to complete a Half Ironman Triathlon the following year, inspired by his new training regime to take on an even greater challenge.

Escaping the Comfort Trap

So how do you know if you're in a comfort trap? Usually, if you're really honest with yourself, you can feel when your growth is slowing down and it's time to take on something new. The exercise at the end of this book may help with this kind of reflection. Life starts to feel a bit too easy or routine, or it begins to lose the sense of meaning and excitement it once had. You may start feeling bored or restless, or find yourself asking, "Is this all there is?" Even with these nagging feelings, sometimes we can be very good at convincing ourselves that where we are is OK, especially if it's comfortable and the alternatives for growth are less comfortable. There are lots of justifications and distractions we can use to reinforce our decision to stay put. When we do this, we end up selling out our dreams in exchange for comfort.

There's only one way to escape from a comfort trap, and that's to let go of what's lulling you to sleep motivationally and take on a new challenge, big or small, to build your confidence. Sometimes it requires a major life crisis to create the impetus to do this. But often a boost from someone who sees your potential (or even a book like this) can be enough to help you realize what you're missing out on and get you back into motion so that you can take the next growth step.

Lisa Pijuan-Nomura (whom we introduced in chapter 3) was a dancer who wasn't dancing. Running a literacy program offered more security with its regular salary, and it was somewhat related to one of her long-time goals of working with children's books. At least it was related enough that she could tell herself it was an OK thing to do and a respectable job.

Then one night she had a dream about one of her dance mentors, a woman named Karen Kaeja. The next day, out of the blue, Lisa received an e-mail from Karen, asking, "What are you doing with your dance?" Lisa replied, "Oh well, you know, I'm not sure how much the world wants to see chubby dancers, and I'm a bigger girl . . ." Karen wrote back and said, "Dance isn't about shape or size, it's about spirit. You have one of the most beautiful spirits, and people in Toronto and the world have to see it."

These words of encouragement and the strange co-incidence with the dream were enough to make Lisa see that she had been hiding behind excuses. If she wanted to be a dancer, she should just go out and do it. In that moment she decided to quit her job and become a full-time performer. Despite her complete conviction that it was the right thing to do, the thought was still terrifying. The dance show she was working on at the time would run for another month and a half, but after that she had nothing planned. Three days before the last performance, she still had nothing new lined up.

Then, on the day of her last performance, something extraordinary happened. She got a phone call from a production company in Ireland looking for dancers for a film. They had heard about her. They would need her in Ireland for two months starting the following Wednesday.

After she got back from that trip, good things continued to come her way. People kept hearing about her and work kept coming. It was as if her decision and conviction had opened the floodgates of opportunity. Her confidence about her ability to do anything blossomed. She discovered that she also had a talent for programming other artists, and quickly made a name for herself as an innovative and successful curator of shows that combine many different types of performance.

Five years later, with a bimonthly cabaret in which to showcase artists and a growing career as a creativity coach, she had become the one providing the opportunity and encouragement for others to take risks they might not have taken on their own. She has continued to challenge herself by becoming a visual artist, and moving to a new city where she has quickly become a fresh voice and respected innovator in the local arts community.

The Growth Is in the Striving

It may sound as if Lisa was just very lucky, but the truth is, no matter what had happened, she would have grown once she made the decision to commit herself wholeheartedly to being a performer. If you take on a new challenge and don't succeed at achieving your goal, you can still grow just as much by transforming the experience into lessons for the next time.

She is fairly candid about the fact that not every day was easy. But her own periods of self-doubt ultimately made her a better coach and a better artist. In fact, her work often draws on the humor, humanity and everyday heroism that we can all relate to in moments of vulnerability and transition. Your own story of becoming who you are (which is always a work in progress) is made much more interesting by the challenges you take on and overcome, especially when these require courage, and when we fight through the uncomfortable parts, proving to ourselves and others that we can.

Those who are used to making their confidence greater than their comfort will tell you that after awhile, you become less fearful of making mistakes. In fact, you begin to realize that the biggest breakthroughs often come from making mistakes, because that's where you get your best improvement ideas. The "courage" phase, with all its discomfort, between making a commitment to do something new and the feeling of accomplishment you have once you succeed, becomes more tolerable once you realize it's the temporary price of growing, and that growth, at least, is guaranteed. No matter how things work out, you'll always grow more and reap rewards from leaving comfort behind and doing things that force you to develop new capabilities and confidence as long as you see them through. You just have to be okay with not always knowing in advance what those rewards are going to be. Where lifetime growth is concerned, always making your confidence greater than your comfort is a no-lose proposition.

Where Do I Start?

● *Use goals to get yourself in motion.* If you know you're stuck in a comfort trap, it's probably time to set some new goals. They can be big goals or small goals. Big goals can be especially inspiring, but you may need to break down a big goal into smaller, manageable, measurable steps in order to know where to start. Small goals are useful because they are easy to accomplish and give us a quick boost in confidence, but you'll need to make sure that you either keep setting new ones or connect them to some larger goal, if you want to stay in motion. Here's a secret about goals: what matters most is not whether you achieve the goal, but that the goal gets you striving, because striving leads to growth. Often the most valuable results are actually unexpected by-products of pursuing other goals.

● *Take a break if you need one.* Sometimes people lose their confidence in the middle of a particularly challenging activity, project, or series of events because they become overwhelmed or exhausted. It's often a better idea to take a comfort break to rejuvenate yourself than to continue to work if you're becoming less and less effective.

After you've renewed your energy and focus, you'll be able to accomplish more in less time and make up for the time you spent resting. If possible, take at least one full day in which you completely disconnect from the source of your stress and do something that gives you pleasure. And remember: discomfort, and the courage it takes to get through it, is a natural part of developing any new capability. Once you get through it, you'll be at a new level and able to enjoy the fruits of your efforts.

- *Use your past as a model.* Here is a case where you can use the past as raw material in a different way, as proof of concept, proof that you've done this before and you can do it again. In Strategic Coach, we have an exercise we call The 4 C's Formula, and one way you can use it is to look at a past experience so you can see how you built a new capability more clearly. Once you see it in one experience it's easy to recognize it in others.

Think of a time in your past where you developed a new capability. The place it starts is with commitment, with a decision to leave your comfort zone and try something new. The next step is courage. You have to get through the fears and unpleasantness that comes with the learning and uncertainty of doing something that stretches you. As you work through this fear, though, you develop new capabilities and those lead to confidence. Look at your own experience and write down what each of those stages looked like for you and you'll see how it worked in the past. Then the next time you have an opportunity to make a commitment to something that requires courage, you'll be able to map out what the process will look like in your mind and be more conscious as you go through the stages. This is especially helpful as you go through the courage stage. Feeling crappy because you're in a courage phase of growth is very different from feeling crappy because you're stuck or stagnant. Being clear on the commitment you've made and the capability and confidence you're working to build won't necessarily take the suffering out of the courage phase, but it will put it into a context that reminds you why what you're going through is worthwhile.

Law Nine

Always Make Your Purpose Greater Than Your Money

Greater purpose is essential for lifetime growth. Many people start off their careers thinking that money is the goal. Money can be a useful measure of success or progress in certain circumstances, and it's a resource we can use to realize greater possibilities, but at some point money without purpose loses its meaning. Money as an end becomes a growth stopper. Having a purpose that is greater than yourself will give you a constant impetus to strive. Purpose gives life meaning and helps us to direct and focus our talents and efforts. It also attracts the talents and energies of others whose purposes align with our own. Think of money only as a means of achieving a greater purpose, and you'll attract all the resources and rewards that make up a rich life, not just money.

Some people might look at this law and think, that's a nice idea, but isn't it a bit idealistic? The answer is no.

Even in the business world, it's quite possible to grow successfully by making your purpose greater than your money.

Where Profit Serves Purpose

When Dan Sullivan and Babs Smith first met, Babs was running a holistic health practice and Dan was coaching entrepreneurs and politicians one-on-one. They both got a lot of energy out of helping people to overcome the obstacles that were keeping them from growing, being happier, and achieving their goals. The two became fast friends, supporting each other's ideas and business development, and as their personal bond grew and strengthened, they eventually joined forces in life as a couple.

Babs could see that Dan's tools and processes had the potential to reach and help a lot more people. She committed herself personally to using her talents and business sense to create an organization that could help this work grow and thrive and reach more people. In her vision, this organization would sustain not only Dan and her, but also the other people who would join with them to help fulfill this purpose; and it would always keep growing, continuing to be viable and sustainable even beyond their lifetimes. This was the initial vision that became The Strategic Coach Inc. Babs concluded her health practice and began to apply her abilities to build this organization around

Dan's work, growing the business that would achieve these goals.

Money was an important part of achieving this purpose and continues to be, in order to fund the growth that allows the work to continue and the full vision to be realized. But it has never been the main purpose, and over the years Dan and Babs have learned how to protect the guiding vision and align their team members behind it. This began with a series of statements they call their "prime directives."

When they started The Strategic Coach Program in 1989, their goal was to make enough money to pay off a large lump sum of back taxes. Although the goal was driven by a need for cash flow, they chose to achieve it in a way that would also further their bigger purpose. They decided to start a workshop program in which Dan would coach a group of entrepreneurs together instead of meeting with clients individually. This allowed them to apply Dan's process to more people, which meant more revenue.

Protecting the Core

It became clear to Dan and Babs, through challenges and opportunities in the growth of The Strategic Coach, that the strength of their personal connection was the most important factor in achieving their bigger goals in life and with the business. To ensure that this would always be protected, they gradually came up with three "prime directives" to guide them as they grew the business. These are as follows:

1. Everything we do has to support our increasing teamwork and intimacy.

2. We will always maintain control over the forward forces of our progress.

3. We will only align ourselves with people who are aligned with us.

As you can see, these points are not a mission statement for the company, but rather a personal value statement of what is important to Dan and Babs for preserving the core components of their personal and business success: their relationship, and the company as an engine of growth. As guidance for business decisions, these directives nipped in the bud many opportunities that seemed potentially lucrative at the outset but might have proved disastrous later. They have removed temptation to make pacts with the wrong people. They have spawned systems to improve communication so that Dan and Babs and the team are kept more closely in alignment. They have shaped a company that is known for its integrity and for walking its talk. And they have allowed the team to join in to support Dan and Babs in preserving their core values and strength as a couple.

The company has grown its revenue by more than a hundredfold since they came up with these directives, and there is always a sense of abundant resources to fund more growth. The team has over 100 more people, and the vision is unfolding in a way that respects, values, integrates, and rewards each team member's unique contribution. The company is reaching more people than ever, and Dan's work is having a tremendous and growing impact on an increasing number of lives. In short, the original bigger purpose is being realized. Money continues to be viewed always as a by-product of the company's efforts to create value by realizing this purpose in ever-greater ways.

Could Dan and Babs have made more money by compromising some of these values? Perhaps in the short term. However, in retrospect it's almost certain that any of the ventures that seemed tempting at the time would have disrupted the organic growth that has since led to much bigger opportunities completely in alignment with their bigger purpose.

When Purpose and Money Clash

Dan and Babs have managed to create a business in which money flows in from their pursuing their greater purpose. This structure has allowed both of them, along with their team members and of course their clients, to grow in many ways, personally and professionally, while making more money. However, it isn't always the case in life that our opportunities to make money are so aligned with our purpose and values. This is where making your purpose greater than your money can seem like a much tougher choice. After all, we need money to live, and the benefits of maintaining a sense of purpose aren't always so clear.

The problem is that, faced with a choice between money and purpose, if we choose money and give up on purpose, it often leads to a trap that stops us from growing. The money can help us distract ourselves from this fact, but the honest truth is that what we will have to show for our efforts is just more money or stuff, rather than personal growth. Without the purpose to put it to good use, more money becomes meaningless. A drop in income is a small price to pay for the rewards you get when you choose to stick to your purpose, as we see from Bryson's story.

Bryson MacDonald is a retired social worker. Early in his career, he took a high-paying job with a car manufacturer as an "employment counselor." Once in the position, he was asked to find excuses for not hiring "ethnics" or women.

Although he had a new family and nothing else lined up, he stuck with his principles and quit.

He'd helped a local halfway house by hiring parolees for the assembly line. ("You can't steal a car that isn't assembled," he jokes.) When the parole office heard he was available, they hired him immediately.

"I took a terrific pay cut," Bryson says, "but it was good for my health." The decision set the tone for the rest of his career, and several ex-convicts still remember "Mr. Mac" as the man who helped them turn their lives around.

Bryson's story shows that purpose doesn't have to be grandiose; it can be as down-to-earth as the commitment to be a good person, as defined by one's own standards.

The Slippery Slope

But what about when there's good money to be made and you just have to compromise a little? Can't you take the money and then go back to having a purpose later? This is a personal choice that may depend on circumstances and the importance of the purpose you're being asked to undermine or ignore. The problem with taking a little payoff is that it can be a slippery slope. Once you compromise your values, they become devalued in your mind, and it seems a little easier to do it the next time ... and before you know it, it's all about money again. The other thing is, what looks like a little compromise when you're staring at a big payoff can seem like a much bigger sacrifice later when you have to live with all the results of your decision.

The Courage to Walk Away

Walking away from money to maintain integrity with your values and sense of purpose forces you to grow. It gives you the opportunity to strengthen your commitment to your values and to use your creativity and ingenuity to find other ways of meeting your financial needs that are more in line with your greater purpose.

Fidel Reijerse was an environmental consultant in the 1990s. The purpose that drove him in his work was the desire to help organizations find ways to get things done effectively while doing less damage to the environment and to people's health.

New building sites often bring together materials that on their own may not be hazardous but in combination can create toxic spaces that are potentially harmful to people and to the natural environment. Add to these toxic substances the increased energy demands and waste-management burdens of a new large-scale building project, and the environmental impact can become substantial.

Like others in the field, Fidel was aware that there were products and solutions on the market that reduced these negative impacts—environmentally preferable products—but these were usually perceived as more expensive. The corporations doing the building were concerned with keeping costs down for their shareholders. Some corporations were willing to do enough to make themselves look like good corporate citizens, but they were very shrewd about where the line was. It became clear to Fidel that the only way corporations would make full use of environmentally preferable products and technologies was if they cost the same as or less than the mainstream alternatives.

What frustrated him was that this was possible. He knew that some of these products could save the corporations money and protect the environment, but this was not what was happening in the marketplace. Many of the companies producing products that are better for the environment take advantage of the premium they can charge and the differentiation that comes from being considered "green." The expectation that you should have to pay more for an environmentally preferable product is actually what keeps these products from being used more widely and hence having a bigger impact on reducing harm to the environment and health hazards to people.

When Fidel realized that neither the corporations nor the producers were willing to go any further, because of where their own interests lay, he decided to leave the consulting business to pursue other projects. A new opportunity had come up that offered a greater potential for his efforts to result in better solutions, and not just more income for doing the same thing.

For the next seven years, Fidel went through a tremendous growth experience that culminated in a unique dilemma when a technology he created to help scientists could not be brought to market in an ethically acceptable manner. The technology has great potential to do good, but also equal potential to do harm if misused. Though it would have been easy to sell out and take a payoff, Fidel and his business partners thought it was more important that they retain control long enough to direct the technology toward positive applications. When it became clear to Fidel that he could no longer be useful in making this happen, he left. Once again, he was looking for a project that would recapture his passion and engage his sense of purpose.

Purpose Finds Opportunity

Freed up, Fidel experienced a rush of creativity and new ideas. The growth in his confidence and capabilities that had come from seven years in another venture gave him access to new insights. Within months, he had figured out a potential answer to the problem that had caused him to leave environmental consulting.

His initial vision was to use the 2010 Winter Olympics in Vancouver as a showcase for a very public demonstration of how it is possible to save money while building and running facilities in a way that is better for the environment. The proof would be in the Olympic speed-skating oval in the city of Richmond, the centerpiece of the games' facilities. Those who could provide technologies and building materials legitimately at prices that would allow the Olympic venue to save money and do better for the environment would be invited to participate. The plan enabled everyone involved to profit—in fact demanded it, since financial viability was what was to be established.

His efforts to pull this together required Fidel to draw on every strategic relationship and resource in his arsenal and forced him to push his creativity and diplomacy skills to new levels. The innovative initiative was well received. In fact, people went out of their way to listen, offer help, and get others on board whom they thought should be a part of this. He had no trouble getting the ear of decision makers. By aligning all their interests—profitability, public image, and the genuine desire to do something good for the environment—Fidel managed to create a situation where all the players' individual purposes could align to support a greater purpose. As the idea, still in its relative infancy, became more public, his attitude was that even if someone else were to step in to try to share in achieving the same vision, it wouldn't matter. His concern was more that the goal be reached, regardless of how it happened.

Fidel's sense of purpose told him when to leave this problem alone, and interestingly it also led him back when the time was right. Out of all these conversations, an image of a much larger opportunity began to emerge. He and his partners began to see that the major obstacle preventing builders and building owners across the country from making renewable energy systems part of their projects was the economics, and that it was solvable. The upfront cost was simply prohibitive, even if the long-term benefits were justifiable. By thinking creatively about the problem and seeing it in a new way, they were able to develop a business model that financed the upfront installation cost of rooftop solar-geothermal energy generating systems and allowed building owners to pay for them gradually through energy savings and power sold back to the grid. Effectively, a building owner could install a system to generate power for their building on their own roof with no upfront cost and own it outright after about 20 years. RESCo Energy, the company Fidel and his partners built, has since gone on to install such systems for many large and high-profile buildings in Canada—projects many times the size of a single Olympic stadium.

This story brings up an interesting point: if growth is what energizes you, in the long run few things are worth doing just for the money. On the other hand, some things are worth doing just for the purpose and the growth, whether or not we get paid for them. However, just because you would do something for free doesn't mean you shouldn't try to find a way to make money doing it. The best possible scenario is when you can do something that moves you in this way and get paid well for it, too. Money in support of purpose helps create sustainable long-term growth.

Searching for Purpose, on Purpose

We cannot end this chapter without looking at the obvious question: What if I don't know what my purpose is? Not everyone has a clear, driving purpose like Dan and Babs or Fidel. Sometimes purpose becomes clearer when it's threatened, as in Bryson's case.

Defining a sense of purpose can be a difficult task. Even those who have achieved a lot often struggle with it. But here's the key: even the act of searching for purpose leads to growth. It causes you to ask questions you wouldn't otherwise ask and look for answers in places where you wouldn't otherwise look, to pay attention to things you wouldn't have noticed before, and to make connections and find meaning where you couldn't see it before. Even if you don't know what your purpose is, you can focus on purpose by searching for it. Finding your purpose becomes a purpose in itself, until it is replaced by whatever you discover your purpose to be. Paying attention to what moves you, what stirs your passion and gives you energy is the starting point. Looking for purpose will always create more growth than looking for money will.

THE LAWS OF LIFETIME GROWTH

Where Do I Start?

- *Listen to your heart and your gut.* Your sense of purpose is more connected to your heart, or to your gut instinct, than to your head. We can often talk ourselves into things where money is concerned, but if it doesn't *feel* right, that's a sign that your purpose may be threatened. A choice can seem logical and sensible, but that doesn't always mean it's the best choice for achieving your desired purpose. Let your feelings guide you to the right objective, and then use your head to figure out how to make it happen.

- *State your purpose in writing.* Creating a statement of purpose is useful in many ways. First, choosing the right words forces you to clearly express your purpose. It's worth the time and effort it takes to make the statement accurate. Again, your gut will tell you if it feels right. People who have found their purpose often report that it feels like they're doing what they were always meant to do. Also, statements of purpose allow others to understand and align with you so that they can help you to achieve your vision. Once your purpose is clear, you'll begin to see that some kinds of situations and behaviors support it and some don't. You can use these insights to create further "directives" like Dan's and Babs's to serve as reminders that help you stick to your purpose when opportunities and temptations arise.

Strategic Coach's purpose statement at the time of the writing of this second edition is expressed like this:

Expanding Entrepreneurial Freedom

Our purpose is to free up entrepreneurs and their teams to thrive and grow in a world of rapid change and unpredictability. We provide practical thinking tools and structures and a growth-oriented community to keep them in the right mindset to make their most valuable and unique contributions, achieve their biggest goals, and enjoy an unparalleled quality of life for decades to come.

It took a bunch of drafts and a lot of input and comments from different members of our team to get it right, but we're happy that it encompasses everything we do, while still being fairly specific. You might be able to see how the tools and ideas in this book evolved out of delivering on this purpose.

Your purpose may evolve over time or you may have different purposes that drive you in different parts of your life. All this is completely normal.

Always Make Your Questions Bigger Than Your Answers

Questions are essential for lifetime growth. As children, when we're all growing at a rapid rate, we ask lots of questions. As we get older, we gradually begin to think we have a lot of the answers. For some people, their entire sense of security and self-image depends on having all the answers—on never being wrong. As a result, these people try to understand everything in terms of what they know. But all growth lies in the territory of the unknown. What we already know is in the past. What we have yet to discover is the future. Always make your questions bigger than your answers, and you'll keep drawing yourself into a bigger future with new possibilities.

There is nothing more powerful than a question. The reason is that the mind can't ignore a question. It may choose not to answer, but the question will still be there, provoking new thoughts. Answers, on the other hand, are closed-ended. You can know them and file them away and never think of them again. They don't require any further thought. That's probably why people find them comforting.

Engaging with a Great Question

Questions open the doors to inquiry, which is how we imagine and discover new possibilities. Growth comes not from having the definitive answer but from the activity of being engaged in the conversation around a great question.

So what is a great question, and how do you make your questions bigger than your answers? Great questions are open-ended—that is, they don't have easy answers. A really great question can keep you thinking and growing for a lifetime.

Dan shares this story:

When I was nine years old, I was walking in the cornfields of my family's farm in Ohio. It was a beautiful, clear late afternoon in winter. The sun was still out, but you could see the moon coming up, and there was snow on the ground. As I walked, a plane flew overhead. Looking up and watching it pass by in this big open sky, I suddenly had an expanded sense that anything was possible, and I thought to myself, "I wonder, how far can I go?"

It was one of those moments you never forget. That plane and the whole scene symbolized something much bigger to me. Getting off the farm. Getting out of that town. Traveling to other places. An overview of things much broader than what I had experienced in my life until then. It was global in scope. That question became the defining question for my life. From that point on, I kept asking myself, how far can I go? And I'm still asking, and still going. Even though I couldn't have possibly envisioned then where I am now, there's really no end in sight, as long as I keep asking that question.

Questions Connect Us with the World

However, a question doesn't have to be of this scale to keep you growing. Any question asked in a genuine spirit of inquiry will help you to grow. If you really want to know the answer, you'll grow just by asking the question—*even if you don't ever get the answer.* This is because questions open dialogue. They connect us with the world in a new way.

When you ask a genuine question and do get an answer, you have new knowledge that usually increases your understanding. That new knowledge can lead to other questions, and it can also lead to new ways of acting, new perspectives, and new confidence.

Jon Singer, an entrepreneur from New Jersey, has tirelessly fundraised and advocated for the rights of children with autism, driven by his passion to provide a quality education for his daughter Rebecca, who has autistic tendencies. He has this great story about an unexpected by-product of his and Rebecca's experiences together when she was younger: Rebecca liked to get up very early, earlier than her mother and her brother, so when she lived at home, Jon, who is also an early riser, would get up and take her to Starbucks so that they wouldn't wake the rest of the family. Like a lot of kids with autism, Rebecca has a tough time being in a new place. But with practice, she was able to be there for 10, 15, and then 20 minutes.

There was a nice young manager, Tommy Sherwood, who was there early and would open the door for them. He would say "Hi" to Rebecca, but she wouldn't make eye contact. Eventually, Tommy went up to Jon one day and wanted to know if he could ask him a few questions about Rebecca, because he had seen that she was struggling in the beginning. He said, "How can I make my associates, my partners in the store, be more sensitive to anybody with special needs?" More questions followed, about autism and about raising children, because he wanted to have kids of his own.

Jon sometimes came in not just with Rebecca but with his six-year-old son as well. Tommy and the Singers got to know each other, and Tommy even supplied coffee for one of the visiting days at Rebecca's school. Then one day he called, very excited: "Jon, you won't believe it. I hired this young adult with autism to work in the store. And he's one of my best workers!"

Tommy went on to tell Jon that a year earlier, an agency had come to him looking to place someone, but after discussing it, they had agreed that the working environment might not be suitable. But after meeting Rebecca, learning more about autism, and seeing what she had accomplished with all the time and effort, he had the confidence to hire Chris when the opportunity arose. He thanked Jon for that.

Later, Jon saw an article about Chris, the young man Tommy had hired, in the newspaper. In it, Chris was quoted as saying that the job at Starbucks had been his first real break. They subsequently promoted him, creating a new title—café manager—and put him in charge of rearranging and organizing the store. He made a great contribution. Jon called Tommy to applaud him, saying, "Look what you did for this guy! He had such a tough life, and because you took the time to want to learn about Rebecca, and learn about these things, you're changing his life." He cannot say enough about Tommy and what a great person he is. And all of this happened because Tommy took the initiative to ask some genuine questions.

So what is not a genuine question? Sometimes people ask rhetorical questions, or ask questions not because they want to know the answer but because they're trying to corral someone into agreeing with their point of view. Questions that are asked with a genuine desire to know the answer, without a preconceived idea of what that answer will be, are good, growth-promoting questions.

Embracing What You Don't Know

To keep asking good questions, you have to give up any fears you might have about not already having the answers or appearing ignorant. However, there's another way to look at this. If you value great questions above great answers, then whether or not you know the answer is immaterial. In fact, the best questions may be those that have no answers at all. Making your questions bigger than your answers means always being open to the possibility that your understanding has some flaws in it and always being willing to entertain the idea that there's a better way to do something than the way you already know. Learning and improvement happen when you're open to these possibilities.

At St. John's College in Maryland, where Dan studied the great books, the teaching method is based on asking great questions. Everyone reads the same book. Then 18 people get together with two tutors in a room, and one of the tutors reads a passage and asks a question about it to start the discussion. The most skilled people at St. John's are the ones who can answer a question with a question. Those people keep deepening the conversation and expanding the question so that it becomes even more comprehensive. After two and a half hours of questions, you've heard all kinds of points of view that you never would have thought of on your own. It makes you humble. You realize that no matter how bright you are, you're never going to have the definitive perspective on anything. Life is created out of everyone's perspectives through a constant conversation.

Approaching life by always asking bigger questions allows you to create for yourself a constant sense that there's always more to discover and greater depth to the things you thought you knew. It keeps you open to all kinds of possibilities for greater learning and increased contribution. It forms the basis for all cooperation, shows the way to better performance, and allows us to have a deeper sense of gratitude, compassion, and appreciation for others. Being a great questioner can make life more fun and can also increase your confidence by making you see that the unknown, while sometimes a source of fear, is also a source of excitement, adventure, and opportunity for growth. Big questions help us to define our purpose and give direction to our lives.

In almost every story in this book you will find a key question, or series of questions, behind the person's growth in that moment. This is because always making your questions bigger than your answers is an essential ingredient for every kind of growth. The question is the one form of thought that always actively leads us out of the past and into a bigger future.

Where Do I Start?

● *Engage your curiosity.* If you're having trouble asking genuine questions, go out and find something new that takes you into an area you know nothing about. Read a book or watch a documentary about a subject you've never explored before. Go somewhere you've never visited. Start a conversation with someone you wouldn't normally talk to. Start or join a discussion group to talk about articles or books you haven't read before, preferably on subjects you know little about. Approach these new subjects with a genuine spirit of inquiry—what Zen masters call "beginner's mind." This will give you lots to ask questions about.

● *Challenge yourself to keep the discussion going.* When you find yourself in a conversation with someone and you both have some time, make it a challenge to try to keep the conversation going by asking great questions. You can even do this with someone you've never met before, like a cab driver or the person sitting next to you on a plane. Really listening to what the other person is saying will give you clues about what to ask next.

And a few great questions you can ask yourself to get you started:

If everything I've done up to now is just the beginning, what's next?

What new habit would I like to create for myself over the next 21 days?

If I had 25 years to do something great, what would it be?

What are the ten achievements I'm proudest of over the past year? What could I do as a next step to build on each one of them?

What is no longer acceptable in my life?

What do I want to do more of in life? What do I want to do less of?

How far can I go?

The Decision to Grow

The decision to grow is a decision to take charge of your own future, but, as you can see from the stories we've shared, it always ends up having an impact that goes far beyond just you. When you choose to grow by acting in alignment with the ten laws, opportunity naturally comes to you, ideas and resources flow to you, and people with the right skills, passions, visions, and connections tend to show up to help you. You naturally become more connected with the world as it responds in these ways to support your growth.

Because of this connection, growth always has a ripple effect. It creates inspiration and learning opportunities for others, as in the case of Catherine's mother, Hilda, and of Tommy Sherwood's encounter with Rebecca Singer. It gives birth to new entities that help others, like Mary Anne Ehlert's Process for Protected Tomorrows and Jonathan Smith's fund-raising Web sites. And it creates new capabilities and visions of what's possible, like Matthew Passmore's *Park(ing)* Day changing the way cities look at public space and Clifford Shearing's insights about power that led to more cooperative approaches to security and policing.

Much of the value created by our growth comes in the form of positive impacts on others that we may not even be aware of. In fact, there may be countless people affected by our growth in ways we may only come to know about by chance, if at all. For instance:

Clifford had an opportunity to return to the farm in South Africa a couple of years after being fired, when the farmer was away in town. As he walked over the hills, he began to hear the words "*inyoni ende*" echoing around him. Meaning "tall bird" in Zulu, this is what the other workers had nicknamed him when he worked there. As word spread of his return, "*inyoni ende*" was being chanted all over the farm. People came from all over and greeted him warmly. He was overwhelmed.

He knew that leaving had had a profound impact on his own life, but it wasn't until that chance return that he realized his unusual act of standing up to the farmer's authority had left a mark on the memories of all those present. In that moment, people who felt powerless under apartheid had briefly seen power shifted in their favor. He had only been trying to teach the farmer a lesson for his own reasons. The bigger impact in terms of the hope or possibility or whatever else each of those people had taken away from the experience was much greater than he had ever imagined—and, he admits, he'll never know what the spin-off effects may have been in their lives.

So one of the great benefits of living in alignment with the laws is that, as we grow in order to make our own lives richer and more meaningful, we also make a significant positive impact on the world. This contribution brings us rewards—encouragement, resources, and opportunities—that in turn help us continue to pursue more growth. Because of this, the more you grow, the easier and more enjoyable it becomes to keep growing. As the growth mindset becomes habitual, the laws become part of your innate wisdom. You can deepen your understanding of them and explore them in new ways as you see that more is possible. These explorations will continue to return greater rewards and opportunities that open up pathways in life you could never have even envisioned without having gone through the growth that brought you there.

A World Based on Lifetime Growth

Now we'll ask you to take a leap of imagination to a much bigger future: Imagine a world where all people and organizations habitually operate according to the laws of lifetime growth. People and organizations in this world are focused on using their rewards to make ever-greater contributions. They build systems and structures that favor cooperation over status, use money to achieve goals aligned with their bigger values, and focus on increasing performance, enjoying applause as a by-product. They are more confident about their capacity to create their own futures based on a sense of purpose, genuine curiosity, gratitude for the many blessings and opportunities that surround them, and a desire to keep on learning, growing, contributing, and enjoying themselves.

In this world there is no sense of entitlement to handouts, but there are many gifts given to people who graciously receive them and use them to grow for their own benefit and the benefit of those around them. Solutions to social problems come from cooperation and combined ingenuity—from the contributions of those who have the needed pieces, pulled together by those whose natural inclination is to ask the right questions to find out what really needs to be done. Individuals feel responsible for their own quality of life and are equipped with the mental tools and habits to turn their visions into reality. They know that their own growth is intimately linked to their ability to continually create value for others.

You might think, so much has to change before this can be true, and you are right. But you can see the glimmer of the possibility of this world in the stories in this book, and in countless other stories that are happening around you as people everywhere, knowingly or unknowingly, act in accordance with the laws of lifetime growth and cultivate a growth mindset. You've seen how each of these people impacts many others, often helping them in turn to grow. You've seen how new solutions have been created, how people have been inspired and motivated to act differently, and how people have found energy and courage they didn't know they had.

A world like this is created when more and more individuals like you make the decision to adopt a growth mindset and grow on purpose: taking the laws to heart, deciding to live this way for their own reasons, making their own unique contributions, and providing positive examples for others along the way. You don't need to know about the laws to do this; you only need to act in the ways they suggest. However, it helps to have the laws as a road map because, just as you may be able to get to your destination by the back roads, it's always great to know where the freeway is. There are resources on the following pages to help. You have the book in your hands. The choice is yours. The future is your property.

Tool

The Growth Focuser

All progress starts by telling the truth.

—Dan Sullivan

One of the most effective ways to maximize your growth is to pay attention to where you're growing and where you're not on a consistent enough basis that you can consciously make more growth enhancing decisions and choices. Here, we combine the principles of Laws One and Two to create a weekly exercise where you get to use your recent past every week as raw material for creating your bigger future.

We suggest doing the exercise weekly, because if you wait any longer, you're likely to forget some of the more subtle examples, and shorter periods may make it difficult to come up with enough examples. However, we've left a blank space so you can change to whatever works best for you.

The exercise asks you to think about and jot down anything you did, big or small, to grow in the way described by each law in the past week. There are bulleted reminders of some of the broader kinds of growth enhancing activities that belong to each law just to help jog your memory. Your own examples will be more specific things you did.

Start by filling in column one. Don't worry if you don't have examples for every law each week. The second column is to record any results you may have seen already from having taken these actions. Fill in this column next. Next, circle the law you're most proud of your progress on this week and also the one you most want to work on next week. For each of these, write down your reason for choosing them and a next action step.

If you happen to be doing this with a friend or in a group setting, sharing these last two points makes for a good conversation. Having a colleague, friend, partner or family member do the exercise for themselves so you can discuss what you're each learning and observing will multiply the power of this exercise exponentially. You gain, both in having to articulate your own observations, and in hearing someone else's on their growth, as well as from the feedback you can offer one another.

To get the most out of this tool, log into lifetime growth.com and use the online version, which will allow you to securely archive your results every week so you can track your growth over longer periods of time. You can also print the exercise form there if you prefer to work on paper.

Example of The Growth Focuser filled in:

The Growth Focuser

Law	Description	Progress	Results
		WEEK, (week, month, etc.)	JULY 12 (date)	JULY 19, 2015 (date)
1	**I made my future bigger than my past by:** • Seeing bigger possibilities • Setting goals • Having new aspirations	• BUYING TICKET FOR DREAM VACATION • SIGNING UP FOR GUITAR LESSONS	• LOOKING FORWARD TO WHAT I'LL LEARN & SEE IN NEPAL • IMAGINING MYSELF PERFORMING AT THE LOCAL OPEN MIKE!
2	**I made my learning greater than my experience by:** • Looking at what worked and what didn't • Using past experience as raw material	• REALIZING THAT IF I LEAVE A BIT EARLIER, I CAN ALWAYS BE ON TIME	• GOT TO ALL MEETINGS ON TIME & MUCH LESS STRESSED LAST WEEK. I'M SURE A FEW OF THE CLIENTS COULD TELL. YAY, ME!
3	**I made my contribution bigger than my reward by:** • Practicing non-entitlement • Contributing because it felt like the right thing to do	• VOLUNTEERING AT THE SCHOOL	• FELT LIKE I DID MY PART & MET A FEW COOL PARENTS I DIDN'T KNOW TOO
4	**I made my performance greater than my applause by:** • Focusing on doing my personal best • Being fully present as the doer	• GIVING MY VERY BEST SPEECH EVEN THOUGH ATTENDANCE WAS POOR	• GOT TO TREAT THIS AS A LOW STRESS DRY RUN FOR THE BIG ONE NEXT MONTH. FOUND A FEW THINGS I WANT TO TWEAK.

5	**I made my gratitude greater than my success by:**	• Acknowledging and thanking others • Appreciating what makes my life possible	• FOCUSING ON HOW LUCKY WE ARE TO HAVE SO MUCH GREAT PRODUCE AT THE MARKET IN THIS DROUGHT EVEN THOUGH IT'S NOT AS GOOD AS OTHER YEARS • THANKING THE FARMERS	• MADE SOME FRIENDS & GOT A FEW FREE TOMATOES. BEST TIME I'VE HAD AT THE FARMERS' MARKET IN A WHILE.
6	**I made my enjoyment greater than my effort by:**	• Turning tasks into games • Engaging with my passion and sense of fun to get results	• CATCHING MYSELF IN TIME TO TRY USING HUMOR W/ THE KIDS TO GET THEM TO AGREE RATHER THAN YELLING AT THEM (MORE FUN FOR THEM & ME!)	• IT WORKED, & I THINK IT MAY BECOME MY GO-TO STRATEGY MORE NATURALLY IN THE FUTURE
7	**I made my cooperation greater than my status by:**	• Multiplying results through teamwork • Getting ego out of the way • Really hearing others	• ASKING JUAN WHAT HE REALLY NEEDS INSTEAD OF ASSUMING I KNEW (I WAS SURPRISED THAT IT WAS SIMPLER THAN I THOUGHT)	• SAVED MYSELF A LOT OF EXTRA EFFORT, & HE WAS REALLY APPRECIATIVE. SAID NO ONE HAD EVER ASKED HIM THAT BEFORE! HE REALLY OPENED UP AFTER THAT.
8	**I made my confidence greater than my comfort by:**	• Taking a risk to create a new capability • Facing my fears • Overcoming excuses	• ASKING PAT OUT ON A DATE • RIDING DOWN & UP THE MOUNTAIN!	• ANSWER WAS YES! WE HAD A GREAT TIME. NERVOUSNESS UNFOUNDED. • RIDE WAS DOABLE & WILL BE EASIER NEXT TIME
9	**I made my purpose greater than my money by:**	• Putting my values first • Seeing money as a means to a greater end	• TURNED DOWN TEACHING POSITION	• FEEL GOOD ABOUT NOT TRADING FREEDOM FOR SECURITY IN THE SHORT TERM. CONFIDENT I WILL MAKE IT WORK.
10	**I made my questions greater than my answer by:**	• Asking a mind-expanding question • Embracing the unknown as a place where all growth lies	• ASKING MYSELF WHERE I REALLY WANT TO GO NEXT W/ MY BUSINESS	• NOT SURE ABOUT THE ANSWER, BUT THE QUESTION HAS ME THINKING ABOUT SOME REALLY INTERESTING THINGS

The Growth Focuser

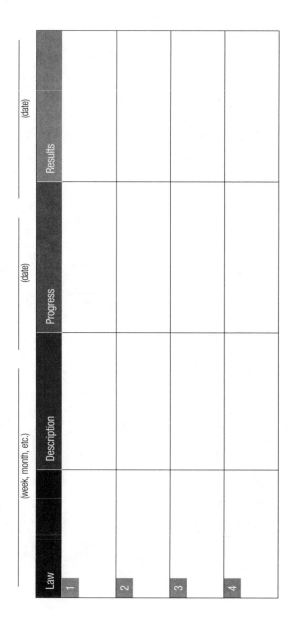

Law	Description	Progress	Results
(week, month, etc.)		(date)	(date)
1			
2			
3			
4			

Acknowledgments

As with the first edition, there are many wonderful and talented people without whom this book could not have been created. We would like to extend our deepest gratitude to these people: To Steve Piersanti, without whose clear vision and direction this project would not have happened and to the editorial board at Berrett-Koehler for giving us this chance to update and improve it in this second edition. To Joe Polish; Mary Anne Ehlert; Lisa Pijuan-Nomura; Matthew Passmore; Gaynor Rigby; Todor Kobakov; Chad Johnson; Tony and Mary Miller; Clifford Shearing; Ruth Samuelson; Jonathan B. Smith; Babs Smith; Bryson MacDonald; Fidel Reijerse; Jon and Rebecca Singer and Tommy Sherwood, for graciously allowing us to use your life experiences to illustrate the laws. We only wish we had room to tell more of your amazing stories, because each one of you could be the subject of a book about growth. To Antonio Pijuan and Dan Taylor, whom the world sadly lost in the time between the first edition and this writing, we miss you and hope you would be happy to see your stories live on in this edition as you continue to live on in our hearts and minds. To Jeevan Sivasubramaniam and his original team of reviewers—Amy Yu, Kathleen Epperson, Ann Matranga, Paul Wright, and Eileen Hammer —for helping this book to find its shape and its heart, and to recent reviewers, Don Schatz, Carol Cartaino, and Kathy Scheiern, for their helpful suggestions for this new edition. To Babs Smith, for her love, support, and wisdom, and for seeing the growth potential in us and constantly creating the conditions that free it up to do the most good in the world. To Paul Hamilton, for using his magic powers to help us to collect stories and pull together all the bits and pieces. To Cathy Davis for being the tool wizard. To Christine Nishino, Shannon Waller, Julia Waller and Marilyn Waller, Kory Simpson, Serafina Pupillo, Hamish MacDonald, and Jonelle Burke for their great support, moral and otherwise, through the process of these revisions. And to the incredibly professional and talented team at Berrett-Koehler, who are always a pleasure to work with in every way.

Index

About the Authors

Dan Sullivan

Dan Sullivan is known worldwide as an innovator and visionary whose ideas have set the standard for others in the entrepreneurial coaching industry. For more than 35 years, he has focused on coaching successful entrepreneurs—helping them to transform their lives and their businesses, and enabling them to achieve continually greater levels of success, personally and professionally.

He is cofounder and president of Strategic Coach Inc. As the main creative force behind the evolution of the Strategic Coach Program, and coach of The 10X Ambition Program, Dan is constantly innovating—creating powerful, practical tools and structures to give participants greater confidence, clarity, capability, direction, and focus as they pursue their goals.

Dan coaches more than 1,000 entrepreneurs every quarter and reads numerous books and articles from top online sources which span topics from history and technology to pop culture and the social sciences. This constant infusion of fresh ideas gives him a unique, evolving global perspective on issues surrounding business and personal growth.

As a highly sought-after speaker and presenter, Dan is known for being "refreshingly outrageous" at times and always thought provoking. He is married to Babs Smith, his partner in business and in life. They reside in Toronto.

Catherine Nomura

Catherine Nomura first developed a passionate interest in growth in the rainforests of Borneo in 1991. An encounter with an indigenous tribe whose traditional existence was being threatened by logging and strip mining fueled a powerful desire to learn how individuals could take greater control over their own futures and grow in a way that would honor their values, unique experiences, skills, and knowledge.

While completing a master's degree in development studies, she began to see that entrepreneurship was a means to self-determination that could offer many opportunities to attain a better quality of life without sacrificing essential values and community ties. After completing an MBA and working with and studying organizations that help people in the developing world to have bigger futures through entrepreneurship, she found herself attracted to Dan Sullivan's uniquely powerful ideas and tools. She joined Strategic Coach in 1998 with the desire to help these concepts find a wider audience.

In the past 18 years, Catherine has helped to find and shape numerous growth opportunities for Strategic Coach. She is coauthor of the books *Unique Ability: Creating the Life You Want* and *Unique Ability 2.0* with Julia Waller and Shannon Waller. Outside of Strategic Coach, she has consulted with entrepreneurs around the world, helping them to turn their growing visions into realities, and is co-founder of kountable, a technology-based company that provides innovative financing solutions to entrepreneurs in emerging economies. Still learning from forests, she lives next to Muir Woods, near San Francisco, California.

About Strategic Coach

Founded in 1988 by Dan Sullivan and Babs Smith, Strategic Coach is an organization that has helped over 16,000 highly successful entrepreneurs from more than 60 industries and 12 countries make quantum leaps in the growth of their businesses and in their quality of life. From the wisdom it has developed by working with this dynamic group of growth-oriented individuals, the company has created a wealth of tools and products to help people, including non-entrepreneurs, to grow by increasing their clarity, focus, confidence, and autonomy.

The company's main offering, the Strategic Coach Program, was the first coaching program exclusively for successful entrepreneurs and remains the industry's gold standard. More than 3,000 entrepreneurs currently attend Strategic Coach workshops in either The Strategic Coach Signature Program with one of our associate coaches, or The 10x Ambition Program with Dan Sullivan on a quarterly basis.

Strategic Coach participants significantly increase their income and time off, while building self-managing, self-multiplying companies that leave their competition behind. Many have set new standards in their industries and made significant contributions to their communities through the increased focus, resources, and creativity they gained by participating in the program. Because of these results, most participants continue to attend Strategic Coach workshops year after year. They comment that as they grow, the program grows with them.

For more information about Strategic Coach, visit www.strategiccoach.com.

Berrett–Koehler
Publishers

Berrett-Koehler is an independent publisher dedicated to an ambitious mission: *connecting people and ideas to create a world that works for all*.

We believe that to truly create a better world, action is needed at all levels—individual, organizational, and societal. At the individual level, our publications help people align their lives with their values and with their aspirations for a better world. At the organizational level, our publications promote progressive leadership and management practices, socially responsible approaches to business, and humane and effective organizations. At the societal level, our publications advance social and economic justice, shared prosperity, sustainability, and new solutions to national and global issues.

A major theme of our publications is "Opening Up New Space." Berrett-Koehler titles challenge conventional thinking, introduce new ideas, and foster positive change. Their common quest is changing the underlying beliefs, mindsets, institutions, and structures that keep generating the same cycles of problems, no matter who our leaders are or what improvement programs we adopt.

We strive to practice what we preach—to operate our publishing company in line with the ideas in our books. At the core of our approach is stewardship, which we define as a deep sense of responsibility to administer the company for the benefit of all of our "stakeholder" groups: authors, customers, employees, investors, service providers, and the communities and environment around us.

We are grateful to the thousands of readers, authors, and other friends of the company who consider themselves to be part of the "BK Community." We hope that you, too, will join us in our mission.

A BK Life Book

This book is part of our BK Life series. BK Life books change people's lives. They help individuals improve their lives in ways that are beneficial for the families, organizations, communities, nations, and world in which they live and work. To find out more, visit www.bk-life.com.

Berrett–Koehler
Publishers

Connecting people and ideas
to create a world that works for all

Dear Reader,

Thank you for picking up this book and joining our world-wide community of Berrett-Koehler readers. We share ideas that bring positive change into people's lives, organizations, and society.

To welcome you, we'd like to offer you a free e-book. You can pick from among twelve of our bestselling books by entering the promotional code **BKP92E** here: http://www.bkconnection.com/welcome.

When you claim your free e-book, we'll also send you a copy of our e-newsletter, the *BK Communiqué*. Although you're free to unsubscribe, there are many benefits to sticking around. In every issue of our newsletter you'll find

- A free e-book
- Tips from famous authors
- Discounts on spotlight titles
- Hilarious insider publishing news
- A chance to win a prize for answering a riddle

Best of all, our readers tell us, "Your newsletter is the only one I actually read." So claim your gift today, and please stay in touch!

Sincerely,

Charlotte Ashlock
Steward of the BK Website

Questions? Comments? Contact me at bkcommunity@bkpub.com.

Certified Sourcing
www.sfiprogram.org
SFI-00453

Certified

Corporation
bcorporation.net